Faith to Grow a Tree

By Mary L. Street

Faith to Grow a Tree

For privacy reasons, some names, locations, and dates may have been changed. Published by Roaring Hope Publishing.

Emphasis within Scripture quotations are the authors own. Please note that the author has decided to capitalize certain pronouns that refer to the Father, Son and Holy Spirit and may differ to other publishing styles. Take note that satan and all related names are not capitalized. The author chooses not to acknowledge him, even if that means breaking grammatical rules.

Printed in the USA, First Edition: April 2026
ISBN Paperback: 979-8-9957663-2-2
ISBN Hardcover: 979-8-9957663-7-7

For more information, or to book an event contact: www.roaringhope.com.

"It's such an honor to write these words about my dear friend Mary and her beautiful new book, Faith to Grow a Tree. We've known each other for over thirty years now. We go all the way back to our college days when we would spend hours together pursuing God and praying for the nations. And are still friends after all of these years.

What makes this book so special to me is that I haven't just read these stories — I've witnessed these moments firsthand. I've watched Mary walk through seasons of uncertainty, heartbreak, but also hope and incredible breakthrough. Time and time again, I've seen God meet her. Not always in the way she expected, but always in His faithfulness. The stories she shares aren't abstract ideas about faith; they have been lived out with much prayer and wrestling. These are testimonies of what it looks like to trust God with mustard seed faith and watch Him grow something strong and lasting.

One of the most powerful threads woven throughout her life and reflected in these pages is the power of forgiveness. I've seen firsthand how choosing forgiveness, even when it's costly, unlocks a freedom that nothing else can. Holding onto pain and resentment only steals joy and breeds bitterness. But when you release it to God, something shifts. Peace is able to fill the space in your life where things feel heavy.

Mary's life has been a living reminder that God is faithful, that His presence truly is everything, and that He will meet you right where you are if you keep leaning in. This book isn't just a collection of stories — it's an invitation. An invitation to trust, to forgive, to believe again, and to plant even the smallest seed of faith.

And I can say with confidence, after 30 years of friendship and witnessing God at work in her life: He grows trees from mustard seeds. I love you, Mary Mare, and I am so proud of you. The seeds of faith you've planted throughout your life are now taking root and growing in the hearts of others."

—**Heather Ferrante**, www.heatherferrante.com
Author of *FREE TO DREAM,* Founder of The Esther Experience

"In a world that often demands instant results, Mary reminds us how the most beautiful growth in life and in the Spirit requires the patience of a seasoned gardener. My wife Darla and I have known Mary for many years, dating way back to our Pensacola (Brownsville) Revival days, and having witnessed the faithful, steady strength of her own journey, I can say with certainty that she does not write from mere theory. Instead, her words are rooted in deep, lived experience grounded in her walk with the Lord.

In *Faith to Grow a Tree,* Mary Street invites us to move beyond 'surface-level' spirituality. She brilliantly illustrates how a mustard seed of faith, when tended with prayer and perseverance, can transform into a life that provides shade, stability, and fruit for others to glean from.

This book is a powerful testament to her life of faith. If you are looking for the encouragement to keep planting when the soil feels hard or for the vision to see the forest within the seed, this book is for you. I strongly recommend that you read this book and then read it again, as it contains life-giving truth that everyone can apply."

—**Keith Collins**, Founder and President
Generation Impact Ministries & Impact Global Fellowship
keithcollins.net and ImpactGF.org

"Mary Street embodies a faith that inspires, which is grounded in God's wisdom and her lived experience. She is the kind of woman who actually walks in the principles she teaches. *Faith to Grow a Tree* reflects the depth of her commitment and the lessons she has integrated into her life and family. If you are looking for honesty, authenticity, and conviction, I highly recommend reading this book. Within the pages, she shares inspiring stories and practical principles that have sparked real breakthroughs. Prepare yourself to be inspired to trust God more deeply, strengthen your relationship with Him, and lead your family with intention, building a lasting legacy rooted in faith."

—**Krystal Zellmer,** Vice President Klemmer (Klemmer.com)
Author of Amazon's Best Selling Book *Life By Intention*

“Mary and I quickly became best friends in college. We have stayed in touch for over 25 years. She is the most genuine, encouraging, and faith-filled woman of God I know. In my heart, I knew her testimony would bring healing to many. I have watched her walk in faith believing that God would supply her needs, fill the aching place in her heart, and move on behalf of those she ministered to even when the outcome seemed impossible. As a result of her unwavering faith, God has moved many mountains, which has always watered the seed of faith in my own heart. This book will break the chains that bind you, build up your faith to move mountains, and bring healing to your heart and life. The exercises at the end of the chapters will help you put your faith in motion. Prepare for healing in ways you never dreamed!”

—**Jennifer** (aka: Jen-Jen)

“Mary is someone I have had the privilege of knowing for more than 20 years. We worked together as missionaries in Tanzania many moons ago! For as long as I have known her, she has consistently lived a life in faithful pursuit of God, in loving service to those around her, and in eager desire to see others equipped and mature in Christ. I am confident the insights she shares in these pages will not only encourage you but also embolden you in your walk with Christ while offering practical steps for your own growth.”

—**Brian Weaver**, PhD
www.strategicglobalimpact.com

“*Faith to Grow a Tree* is a beautiful and honest invitation to nurture the small seeds of faith that lead to lasting transformation. Mary Street writes with rare vulnerability, wisdom, and hope, guiding readers through healing, forgiveness, hope, and trust in God with practical tools and heartfelt stories. Her words carry both tenderness and authority; this is because it is born from a life faithfully lived in surrender to the Lord and in perseverance. This book will encourage anyone longing to grow deep roots of faith in God and live a legacy that flourishes for generations to come.”

—**Hayley Braun**, Pastor at Bethel Church
Author of *Surrendered To The Holy Spirit,* hayleybraun.com

Author's Note and Disclaimer

This book is written from my personal heart journey and years of experience as a licensed minister who has helped many people walk through heart healing, inner freedom, and personal transformation. The prayers, teachings, stories, and reflections shared in *Faith To Grow A Tree: How Small Seeds of Faith Can Transform Your Life and Grow a Lasting Legacy* are powerful, faith-based tools designed to help you grow in trust and confidence, release unforgiveness, and discover empowerment, purpose, freedom, and hope.

While these principles and prayers have brought healing and breakthrough to myself and many others, this book is not intended to replace professional counseling, therapy, medical treatment, or mental health care. If you are walking through trauma, grief, or deep emotional pain, I encourage you—especially as you participate in the inner-healing prayers—to also seek support from a qualified (preferably Spirit-filled) therapist, psychologist, or counselor as needed.

The purpose of this book is to help you step into the fullness of who God created you to be. You will learn to release what no longer serves you, plant small seeds of trust, and unlock the greater faith that leads to lasting transformation and legacy.

My prayer is for these pages to become a safe and sacred space where your mustard-seed faith grows stronger. May your heart find healing, and may you step confidently into your God-given purpose and build a lasting legacy.

Dedications

To My Four Precious Children—Hope, Faith, Naomi, and Luke:.

Next to Jesus and your daddy, you are my greatest joy. This book is a testimony that no dream is too big and no journey is too hard. Remember that with God, *all things* are truly possible! I dedicate this book to you. You are my first ministry, my greatest delight, and the living legacy I have the honor of watching grow and unfold daily before my very eyes. You are my reason to keep showing up no matter the valley or mountaintop. You helped grow me into the woman I've become as I leaned into being your Mama. My desire to see you show up fully yourselves as you grow made me choose to fight for greater freedom and show up to be fully myself and step into the gold, the giftings God has placed in my life, and going after more (there is always more in life and in God). I have great hope for you, believing my ceiling will become your floor as you lean into Jesus. This will unlock and build toward a greater legacy than what your dad and I have ever given you. I love each of you so much, more than mere words can say. You are my heart, forever and always.

To Your Children (My Future Grandchildren) and the Generations Yet to Come:

May you walk boldly in the purpose God has written over your lives, carrying the wisdom and faith of those who have gone before you.

To My Spiritual Sons and Daughters:

Past, present, and future, may you always know that you are seen, you are chosen, and you are deeply loved by the Father and by me. May you always stay hungry for *the more* of God. There is always more! May your lives roar with hope, love, courage, compassion, and Kingdom vision, lighting the way in this beautiful world for others to follow and forever building God's Kingdom on earth as it is in Heaven. May He get His great reward!

Contents

Foreword

by Steve Backlund

In the stillness of reflection, I've often stood in awe of how God births greatness from the smallest seeds. When Jesus spoke of the mustard seed, He wasn't just giving a parable, He was unveiling a Kingdom mystery. *What begins unseen, buried beneath the surface, carries within it the power to transform lives and leave a lasting legacy.* Faith, even in its smallest form, holds exponential potential. That same divine mystery has unfolded in Mary's life, and this book bears witness to it with profound beauty and grace.

As cofounder of Igniting Hope Ministries—and as one privileged to walk part of Mary's journey—I've seen firsthand the fruit of her steadfast faith. During her season of serving with us in the ministry and since then, I have watched her grow, through both the fire and the fragrance of the process. Her story is not one of quick victories or instant miracles, but of courageous endurance—faith forged in the crucible of pain and refined through seasons of surrender. In a culture of instant gratification, Mary reminds us that Heaven's growth often happens in the slow unfolding of trust that catapults us into greater faith.

Faith to Grow a Tree is not simply a title; it's a testimony. The pages you hold, mirror the very heartbeat of a woman who chose to believe when belief cost something. Mary writes as one who has wrestled and prevailed, as one who has planted her tears and reaped hope. Her words are both an invitation and an impartation, inviting us into deeper surrender and imparting faith that moves us from theory into transformation.

Through Scripture, revelation, and the lens of lived experience, Mary opens the reader's eyes to a greater reality: that God is always cultivating legacy in the hidden places. She calls us to release what hinders, to forgive what wounds, and to say *yes* again to the slow, sacred work of the Holy Spirit. This book isn't a manual; it's a meeting place between your heart and Heaven's invitation.

As you turn each page, expect something to awaken. Mary's prayers don't echo from a distance; they breathe with the nearness of the Holy Spirit. They carry the sound of healing and the fragrance of hope. I have seen the Holy Spirit move in my own journey in similar ways—from early pastoral struggles to joy-filled breakthroughs, where even the small steps of obedience rippled outward, equipping thousands to be transformed through higher beliefs in God and in themselves again.

Beloved reader, I believe this book is your invitation to *roar with hope.* If fear has pruned your dreams too harshly, let these words be the rain that restores them. Let them soften your soil and be a catalyst to help move you into higher beliefs, all while unlocking greater faith. As Paul writes in Romans 12:2, "Be transformed by the renewing of your mind." These pages will do exactly that: they will renew, refresh, and resurrect.

If hope has been dormant in your heart, turn these pages gently and keep reading. Let Mary's faith help awaken your own. Let her story remind you that no valley is too deep, no promise too delayed, and no seed too small for God to bring forth abundance. As she dedicated this book to her children and to her spiritual sons and daughters, I offer my own blessing to you:

Like the tree in Psalm 1, rooted by streams of living water, may your faith grow tall, bearing much fruit. So, step boldly. Your tree is rising. The wind of Heaven is already moving through its branches. It's time to grow a legacy!

With unquenchable joy,

Steve Backlund
Cofounder and Revivalist, Igniting Hope Ministries
Author, *Fully Convinced: The Art of Decision Making*
Church and Business Strategist and Encourager
www.ignitinghope.com

Introduction

In churches across the world there is a timeless, shared message on mustard seed faith. If you are like me and grew up in church, you know exactly what I'm talking about. If the mustard seed faith message is preached in a mundane way, it can sound like a sour violin, but on the other hand, it can be a message infused with Kingdom power to bring you into the fullness of who God created you to be. Power: that's the message I want to release over you as you read this book. Inside each one of us is a measure of faith that we are born with, and that faith is called, you guessed it...mustard seed faith. This itty-bitty faith nudges us to take risks and start with small steps of trust in a faithful and loving God. Believing in something that's hard to fathom, see, or touch may seem pointless. But as we build our muscle of mustard seed faith, slowly it grows roots, and day by day builds within us the foundation for greater faith.

Faith starts small like a mustard seed, yet can function as a compass when we choose to grab hold of it. In the journey of life, our faith compass leads us through valleys of uncertainty and doubt. Often, the sheer vastness of the life we were born into can try to keep our little seed of faith from growing—especially if we suffered emotional or physical abuse or endured trauma as a child (or even as an adult). Sometimes the steps to pursue healing or go after our aspirations and dreams can feel overwhelming, leaving us hesitant to take the first step and activate that mustard seed faith. But doing so leads to trust and breakthrough.

This is where I believe the Kingdom concept of "mustard seed faith" comes into play. It's the idea that choosing to start with small steps of trust can eventually lead to remarkable growth and huge accomplishments in your life. Just as a tiny mustard seed can grow into a large, sturdy tree with a strong anchored foundation in its root system, so can our faith grow, blossom, and be strong. We can have a powerful, steady foundation, no matter our upbringing or the hand we were dealt as a child. Let's be honest, many of us feel like we were dealt a very crappy hand.

When our mustard seed faith is nurtured, we find ourselves stepping into a place of trust in a good God. We find ourselves trusting the process, being open, patient, persistent, and having a new willingness we didn't have before. The seemingly insignificant mundane, day-to-day things we step out in and continue to do can create a faith within us to grow a tree. It's all in the stepping. When we powerfully rise up, no matter how we feel, daily choosing to put one foot in front of the other, our faith can grow a tree. Our faith has the ability to be like a mustard tree, whose roots are deep and whose branches have spread upward and outward, far and wide, massive in all its glory. The strong foundation in its root system makes it a place where people come to find rest.

At the heart of the mustard-seed-faith concept is the famous parable that's been preached over and over again for thousands of years, and it was first initiated by Jesus Christ Himself in Matthew 13:31–32:

He presented another parable to them, saying, "The kingdom of Heaven is like a mustard seed, which a man took and sowed in his field; and this is smaller than all other seeds, but when it is full grown, it is larger than the garden plants and becomes a tree, so that the birds of the air come and nest in its branches."

In this parable, Jesus compares the Kingdom of God to a tiny mustard seed, but when sown and cared for, this little speck grows into a tree so large that birds find shelter in its branches. This simple yet profound analogy illustrates the transformative potential of even the smallest of faith-filled actions. Just as the mustard seed starts small and grows into something significant, our faith journey to trust, to heal, to walk into freedom, to build, etc., also begins with what can feel like insignificant steps. Faith looks like trust. Can you lean in and trust Him in the process of your journey? Friend, when you do, you will grow your mustard seed of faith into a powerful, strong tree and become the powerful person you were created to be.

Now for some fun facts, and this is me just geeking out here, so bear with me! As I was reading about a real mustard seed, I learned that it not only grows into a massive tree reaching up to 30 feet tall to provide shade and branches for covering and nesting for birds, but it also has incredible natural medicinal benefits found in the seeds and in the fruit it produces.

Did you know that both the seed and fruit can be consumed as nutritious supplements? You may be thinking...*No way!* Well, me too. But before I go on, a little disclaimer: I am not a doctor! Make sure you do your own research. Anyhow, I was shocked when I did some research on the mustard tree and discovered its natural benefits. God is the most intricate, cool Creator who never ceases to amaze me.

Let me take a food detour for a moment. How many of you

actually like mustard? I do! I used to like it a lot on cheese sandwiches and bologna sandwiches (which I ate as a kid, many times because it was all we had).

What's cool, is that both the seed and the fruit of a mustard tree can be eaten raw or used as ingredients in different foods and cuisines. The seeds have been known for their abundance in dietary fiber as well as vitamins A and C, calcium, iron, potassium, magnesium, and selenium. In places like the Punjab regions of India, dried mustard fruits are popular flavor enhancers in food and appetite boosters, but not just in India. This is known even around the world. Most often, mustard seeds are used as a cream or just as individual seeds. Mustard is used as a condiment in USA cuisine for things like our traditional Fourth of July hamburgers and hotdogs and in other countries too. I mentioned India already, but there are many other places like Bangladesh, the Mediterranean, Northern and Southeastern Europe, Asia, the Americas, and in Africa, which makes it one of the most popular and widely used spices and condiments in the world.

Now, again, just to reinstate this, I'm no doctor, so do your own research. But the fact that it's medicinal in nature is amazing as well. In my research, I found several notable medical conditions that mustard can potentially help with, including:

- Blood disorders like hypertension
- Headaches and migraines
- Rheumatism
- Asthma

I just find this so remarkable. God gave us plants and trees for our nourishment and for our healing (Ezekiel 47:12), and out of all the plants in the world, He compares the Kingdom of Heaven to a tiny mustard seed—the tiniest of all plant seeds. It says in Matthew 17:20, with this kind of faith we can move mountains.

I believe with this kind of faith we can walk into trust and step into our destiny through greater faith. With any mountain standing in our way, we have the power and authority to speak to it through our faith in Christ Jesus. We get to choose to trust Him; we choose faith in Him. We get to partner with Him to see the breakthrough. Mustard seed faith is stepping out and trusting that the process is good. It is trusting and being comfortable with the fact that it's okay to start small and to take those small steps. Taking small steps requires us to embrace the process and trust the journey we are on.

With any mountain standing in our way, through our faith in Christ Jesus we have the power and authority to speak to it.

In the microwave kind of world we live in, especially here in the USA, more often than not, it pushes the need for instant gratification. However, mustard seed faith encourages us to put one foot in front of the other, to value the journey, and to celebrate the growth process that comes from being patient, persistent, daily walking with God. We do not always need things instantly. Just as a seed needs to die first then time to germinate and grow, our faith needs time to develop and strengthen itself into a strong foundation. It develops as it's regularly tried and tested in risk and in the valley seasons of our lives.

Mountain tops are fun, but the valleys are where our faith muscles grow. God sees our small sacrifices in the valleys and even the small steps of trust. He sees! Every act of trust and belief serves as nourishment, like water for our mustard seed of faith to grow, and this catapults us into greater faith. This kind of faith creates moments and milestones that mark us and lead us into greater growth and builds a firm foundation in God. This kind of faith can withstand any obstacle, including life's storms.

It's so important to celebrate the mustard seed faith within us and the milestones along the way that have built greater character and trust in us. Each milestone is fuel for continued growth and that deserves to be celebrated because it means we are deepening our roots, growing branches, and growing the foundation of our tree.

What milestones of trust have you had to walk through?

By acknowledging and appreciating these milestones, we celebrate and reinforce our faith in a faithful God and our belief in our journey while encouraging ourselves to keep moving forward. Let me ask you again in a different way:

What milestone of trust have you had to walk ***out****?*

Have you pursued healing from trauma? If so, then it is time to celebrate that milestone! I have too. Have you pursued transformation in your family legacy so as to not repeat unhealthy, and sometimes downright demonic, family patterns? If so, celebrate! I have too. Have you pursued a dream, possibly failed, but got back up and ran at that Goliath again? If so celebrate! I have too. Have you stepped into forgiveness in the midst of a broken relationship? If so, celebrate! I have too.

Maybe you're still in the middle of walking them out. Why not celebrate that you are holding this book and that you're ready to move forward, take risk with your mustard seed faith, and walk into greater growth! These moments of celebration provide us with the motivation to continue putting one foot in front of the other, no matter how frustrating, hard, or steep the path may seem. Friend, I believe you can do hard things! It may hurt, but you've got this. Do not stop now; keep moving forward!

All these actions and more are faith milestones worth celebrating. You stepped out into mustard seed faith. Like me, you are showing up, you are leaning in, you are allowing your valleys—which sometimes are deep wounds—to be your training ground where you come out with scars. And friend, those scars become your badges of honor throughout life when you let them. When you walk out of the valleys and run at your Goliaths and overcome them, those scars from those battles now become your place of authority to step into greater faith, to spread your wings, and to grow even more with as your tree branches spread even wider. In these places where you step up and step out, this is where you can lead others into great freedom and help them walk into their own victory.

Just as birds find shelter in the branches of the mustard tree, our mustard seed faith can have unexpected and far-reaching impact to those around us. The small steps we take today in trust not only contribute to our personal growth, but can shift your sphere of influence by inspiring and uplifting others around you. Our actions, no matter how big or small, can create a ripple effect that touches lives beyond our immediate circle. Who is waiting on you to pursue breakthrough and to step into your mustard seed faith?

History is full of stories about individuals who began their journeys with small, unassuming steps of faith, even as non-Christians, and then they went on to do incredible things like start amazing, world-wide companies. Some are entrepreneurs who started in garages like Steve Wozniak, Steve Jobs, and Ronald Wayne who founded Apple. When it started, the company was formally called Apple Computer, Inc. and focused solely on computers. It was founded on April 1, 1976 by college dropouts. Let me say that again just in case it didn't register...they were college dropouts! It's *never* too late.

These guys had a dream and wanted to design computers small enough for consumers to have them in their homes and offices. As the legend goes, the first Apple computers were made in their family's garage in Los Altos, California. Now, as of 2026, Apple computers have a net worth around 3.8 to 3.9 trillion-dollars...a company started in a garage. Wow! That's mind blowing to me. The garage it was founded in is now listed as one of the city's historic properties. Their garage-sized dream went on to impact the world, literally. Now, practically every house in the USA has Apple Computer products in it, and I would even dare to say that every *country* has Apple computer products in it too.

These three men may or may not have known God, but their dream went global because they chose to step into mustard seed faith and trust the process. I'm sure they had some pretty hard, frustrating days, and people may have even made fun of them. Their valleys were real, yet they fought. They didn't quit. They dared to let their mustard size seed of faith carry them. They choose to step into trust, and in time, they became a massive mustard tree—one so big that their branches of faith in a dream extended into homes, into many countries of the world, and reached a global scale. Let that sink in.

Steve Jobs and his friends weren't the only ones who changed the world. There were artists such as Grant DeVolson Wood who began with a single stroke of a brush. He is particularly well known for his portrayal of the American Midwest in his masterpiece *American Gothic*, which has become an iconic example of early 20th-century American art. Grant was a key figure in the Regionalist art movement, infusing subtle humor into his artwork. Grant Wood captured the isolation of modern life. His art became known far and wide. He came to be regarded as one of the three primary artists of American Regionalism. When He sat down or stood to paint what some would have probably considered a silly picture, I'm sure he never dreamed that little old him born in 1891 would paint a money-making picture that's still famous today. It takes that mustard seed faith, stepping out, and taking one step at a time.

People throughout history have changed their entire family legacy because they chose to trust God with simple, mustard seed faith. They sought healing and breakthrough, as did I, along with countless other heroes and heroines mentioned in the Bible. Later in this book, I will touch on a few of these biblical figures, all of whom exemplify the power of mustard seed faith. Their stories remind us that greatness is not achieved overnight. Greatness is the result of recognizing that stewarding your mustard seed of faith well, stepping into trust in God, consistent effort, and unwavering belief bring greater faith that moves the mountains.

As a Christian, we hold the belief that *with God all things are possible* (Matthew 19:26). You may not be able to see down the road into tomorrow, next week, next month, or even a year from now, but that is okay. You do not need to see it yet because it's about what you do now and the steps you take TODAY that matter most.

One of the primary challenges we face when we start pursuing our dreams and reaching our full potential is the intimidation we feel when we try to envision the bigger picture. This intimidation is usually caused by fear. We often underestimate our abilities, thinking we aren't good enough, knowledgeable enough, or we'll never be wealthy enough to start the business, go after that dream, etc. We become discouraged by the magnitude of the task at hand and by the lies we fight in the battleground of our mind and heart. We allow self-doubt to sabotage our thinking, which paralyzes us from success and generally holds us back. We get stuck in our own prisons of faithless endeavors, projects unfinished, broken dreams unaccomplished, and relationships un-mended because of our lack of faith to trust God.

Simply put, it is exhausting. It starts to feel like we're on a Ferris wheel, spinning around and around, constantly tired from the continuous and senseless daily grind. Mustard seed faith, however, teaches us that we can jump off the Ferris wheel. The truth is, we don't need to just grind or feel stuck, and we certainly don't have to have all the answers or resources we need right from the start. By taking small steps, we can gradually build our confidence and overcome the fear of failure that often accompanies ambitious goals and dreams.

> The truth is, we don't need to grind or feel stuck, and we certainly don't have to have all the answers or resources we need right from the start.

My life is full of mustard seed faith moments—from the time I was little to now as an adult. I have learned that a heart fortified by faith sees life's obstacles as opportunities for growth. If you personally know me, you will hear me often say, "When you choose faith, even if you only step in with mustard seed faith, *everything is an invitation for growth, breakthrough, and greater intimacy with God.*"

In the face of adversity, faith becomes a shield, reminding us that even in our weakest moments, there's a divine force carrying us forward. His name is JESUS, the one and only true *Jesus Christ of Nazareth who came in the flesh.*

Throughout the rest of this book, there are stories from my life and from the lives of others that I pray will inspire you to harness the mustard seed faith inside of you and trust in a good God. God can and will help you grow a tree of legacy and will do the impossible in and through you, no matter what you have been through. He *is* the God of all hope. Romans 15:13 says,

Now may the God of hope fill you with all joy and peace in believing, so that you will abound in hope by the power of the Holy Spirit.

As one of my spiritual mentors Steve Backlund says,

"You have permission to be hopeless about anything God is hopeless about."

Think about that for a minute. Is God hopeless? Friend, if you can answer *yes*, then I challenge you to go after the lies you're believing. The belief in those lies keeps you from stepping into your mustard seed faith and walking into all that God has for you. From the time I was a child, lies were instilled into me of hopelessness; however, God repeatedly showed up and showed Himself faithful. California is the state where I was born and raised, and at times, things were hard. Life felt hopeless to me during different seasons of my adolescent years. Yet, looking back, I can see how God fought for me to step into truth in my innermost being as I trusted Him.

As you continue to read, I want to invite you into that same place I leaned into within myself—the place of trusting God and walking into hope. Let me take you into the memories and stories where mustard seed faith was ignited in my own life. It's time to go after the lies, step into your mustard seed faith, and see truth come alive in your innermost being. It's time to build a healthy core of who you were made to be. Becoming healthy from the inside out helps you step into the mustard seed faith, which then catapults you into greater faith to harness your future. Do you want to grow? I believe as you keep reading, your life will be challenged, and as you lean in, growth will happen.

Are you ready? *Let's go!*

Chapter 1

California Dreaming

It was a cool, crisp, California day in December—in the late-80s. I can't remember the exact year; however, I can remember the day. The colors were brilliant, with the bluest blues and wisps of white clouds scattered across the morning sky. The sun had broken through, spilling out beautiful golden rays of light that California mornings are so famous for. The light seemed to dance off the clouds while breaking into the atmosphere around me. Looking back now, it was as if the rays of sun were singing praises to God, all the while boldly showing off His great artistry. I can remember it as if it were yesterday, and while I should have been happy, in my heart, I was actually feeling pretty bummed out and downright sad.

Christmas was around the corner—just days away—and as usual my mother had no money to buy us Christmas gifts. She was a single mother of six kids, and five of us were still living at home. At age 11 or 12, most kids are bursting at the seams, fully expectant and excited at Christmas time, counting down the days until fun, wrapped presents come their way. For me, unfortunately, it wasn't in my little girl heart to be cheerful or happy. I was so used to being told that we didn't have enough money, and honestly it was true. I had lost hope, and my heart felt numb.

This particular year, the one thing I dreamt of and really, really wanted was a Walkman. Not just any Walkman either...I wanted a purple one. Why purple? I have no idea, but that's what I really wanted: a purple Walkman.

Of course, I'm totally dating myself, as some of you reading this probably don't even know what a Walkman is. Well, let me educate you and take you back into the old-school history books of music devices for a minute. When I was a kid, cassette tapes were all the rage. You listened to music recorded on the cassette tapes and could even record songs off the radio (or your own recordings) and re-listen. A Walkman was a portable cassette player with headphones. It had a rewind, fast forward, pause, and play buttons, and it ran on batteries. It was like the modern-day iPod or iPhone playing the latest playlist of my childhood days and was so cool, or so I thought!

I can remember my mother having one cassette tape we'd listen to a lot—a Christian music artist back in the late 80s and early 90s. His name was Chuck Girard. I loved music and wanted this Walkman *so* bad. I didn't want to *borrow* one, I didn't want a used one, I wanted my own! Deep in my little girl heart, buried inside the walls of broken promises and disappointment, I totally believed it wouldn't happen because the same words haunted me day in and day out: "We don't have enough money!" Little did I know, God knew the deepest desires of little Mary. He knew the desires of my little-girl heart, and He cared!

So, here we were, Christmas right around the corner, and there was a knock at the door. Running to look out the window, I saw a brown UPS truck parked in front of our little rented house. It seemed to have just showed up out of nowhere at the house where we were staying at the time. Quizzically, we opened the door, and there was the UPS guy in his brown uniform with a big smile and boxes. "Hello! MERRY CHRISTMAS," he bellowed. Beaming smile and a clipboard in hand, he waited for a signature to show that we had received the packages. My mother took the clip board (yup, nothing digital back then) signed for the two boxes, thanked the guy, and shut the door.

All of us kids were excited to see what treasures the boxes held. She sat the boxes on top of the table and began to open them one at time. It felt like forever, our eyes popping out of our heads in anticipation. There, in the boxes, were beautifully wrapped Christmas presents. It seemed that time stood still, all of us in shock. However, hardly any time passed before *another* UPS truck showed up. I think it was two or three trucks that came that day, one after another, and suddenly a ton of brown cardboard boxes filled the floor. Soon, under our Christmas tree were pretty wrapped presents. There were presents of all different shapes and sizes, wrapped in vibrant Christmas colors.

An aroma of hope and joy began to stir in us—especially me—and looking back, it was a mustard seed faith that permeated the environment around us, which was simply not the norm in our household. The mountain of surprise presents seemed to spill out from under the tree, but in reality, at that age you don't take into account there were five of us kids. Of course it would have seemed like a bazillion gifts!

We were in awe of these wrapped Christmas packages, and each gift had one of our names on it. To this day I will never forget what was written on the gift tags. "To: Mary..." "To: Selina..." "To:

Daniel..." "To: Ruth..." "To: Becky..." And all of them said they were from Jesus. What? From JESUS? Our minds were blown.

Looking back, I remember a feeling of love fill the room, and something was ignited in my heart that day. Several boxes had my name on them, but to this day I can't tell you what was in most of them that Christmas morning, other than the one present that made time stand still in my little-girl world. You can probably guess what I'm going to tell you! Yep, on Christmas Day I opened one box with a beautiful purple Walkman in it! All mine...from Jesus. Choked up with tears, I remember thinking, *Wow...He DOES care!*

Looking back, I can remember feeling love fill the room. Something was ignited in my heart that day.

For a long time, we didn't know who had sent those gifts, but years later, as the story goes, supposedly our names as a "family in need" were given to that Christian artist we had a cassette tape of—Chuck Girard and his wife. God had moved on their hearts to bless us. Little did they know their trust in God to step out in faith and bless our family in that Christmas season would be a beginning of mustard seed faith ignited in my little-girl heart, leading to me trusting God in a deeper way and unlocking crazy faith in my life. Little did I know that years later, it would still be building a legacy of faith for my family and for others around the world. For the first time in my albeit short life, little Mary felt seen, and I felt allowed to hope again. I saw a glimpse of God, not as a Judge but as a good Father.

Seeing God as good was always a struggle for me. In my early childhood days, I remember feeling afraid of God. I was told He was my Heavenly Father full of love, but instead, it felt like He wanted to smite me. This was all due to my upbringing and the religious spirit I lived under. I formed the belief that God was a big mean King, who seemed more like a scary Judge who expected me to be perfect or else He wouldn't love me. If I did anything wrong, I thought I would get in trouble and go to hell. Surely, He was mad if I made any mistakes. As a little girl I had a very sensitive heart. I longed for nothing more than to be loved by Him and loved and liked by people, but was this really possible? Did He really care?

That day on the beautiful, sunny, crisp December morning, I had a glimmer of hope. *He not only cares, but He loves me too.* The small mustard seed of faith was activated and started to sprout in my heart. That day, I began to trust again. A little glimpse of hope helped me believe I am loved and I can trust in this good and loving God.

Seeds, if well cared for, well-watered, and have plenty of sunlight, give life. They grow into hearty plants or trees, which over time have the potential to produce amazing fruit (like the mustard tree I talked about in the introduction). The seed planted on that December morning forever will be etched in my memory and heart, yet little did I know that it would be tried and tested many times in the midst of life's trials and valleys I had yet to walk through. No matter what, I knew there was hope!

Are you at a place where it feels hard to trust God? What circumstances in your life have skewed your perception of Him as a good, good Father? For me, life hasn't always been full of roses. There have been many valleys of struggle—too many to count in all honesty—yet there were still mountain tops which caused my mustard seed of faith to grow, developing deep roots within me. Every now and then, God would send people across my path to release glimpses of hope that watered the seed more and more.

The valley seasons of life are not easy, as many of you know. There were times in those seasons I wanted to throw in the towel. My vision of Him wasn't always clear. The way we see God will determine the shape of our faith. We all see through certain lenses of life, and sometimes those lenses are tainted by the junk we go through as a child and even as adults. We all are like plumbing pipes. Pipes, when they're brand new, are smooth inside, and any water that's poured through them flows freely. But when a pipe has years of usage, corrosion builds up on the inside, and it's much harder for water to flow through it purely. As children, we start out like those clean pipes. We start out with pure hearts, which is why many children, in my opinion, can easily see in the realm of the spirit; they see angels and more. Children just seem to encounter our Heavenly Father easier.

My son Luke at six years old would tell me of the angels he saw at different times. Sometimes he saw black angels, and we had to walk through breaking off fear. We taught him that God in him is all powerful and that He has given us authority over the enemy. We taught him that because of Jesus in him, his words are powerful too, and all he had to do is rise up in his Kingdom authority and use them. He caught on really quick.

One night, he was afraid to go to bed because of the "black angels" that apparently, according to him, kept coming only at night. So, I told him to use his words and tell them to "Go back to where you came from IN THE NAME OF JESUS CHRIST OF NAZARETH." He proceeded to walk to our front door, open it, and yell that at the top of his lungs, adding, "And don't you ever come back again!" Well, that night and every night since then, he has slept like a baby. At other

> If we don't allow God to do spiritual heart surgery in us, then we will never experience life the way we were created to live it.

times, he saw white angels and he felt joy and love. He is ten now and still has angelic encounters from time to time with "white" angels. He shares about these encounters so matter of fact, like they're no big deal to him; they are so normal in his day-to-day life.

I never had this kind of perception at his age. At a young age, my pipes so to speak were already becoming blocked up. The enemy was already creating a buildup of debris within me. Looking back, there was a real battle over my life, and he wanted to make sure I couldn't see the Heavenly Father rightly. Yet just like the purple Walkman day, there would be moments when God would break through. I could feel and sense Him around me.

I'm so convinced, that the Holy Spirit, at times, can move and flow easier through children than He can through us as adults. Children are often without hesitation, and they can more easily step into the mustard seed faith. I believe this is why in Matthew 18:3–4 Jesus says,

Truly I say to you, unless you are converted and become like children, you will not enter the kingdom of Heaven. Whoever then humbles himself as this child, he is the greatest in the kingdom of Heaven.

Children have a pure faith, which equals pure, raw, Heavenly Kingdom power. They simply trust and believe. As time goes on, and we grow from children into teens then young adults and adulthood, we end up dealing with junk we've accumulated throughout those different stages of life. Some of us deal with more junk than others, having experienced real disappointments, trauma, and pain, making it feel harder for us to simply step into trust and belief. Our hearts get filled with corrosion, and we grow walls to "protect" ourselves. We lose the little girl or little boy inside who simply believed. We lose the little child inside who simply laughed, simply dreamed, simply danced, simply played, or simply trusted. We lose the child who was goofy or who simply smiled at life and was simply *free*.

Have you lost your childlikeness?

For many years I did, and I had to step into that mustard seed of faith and allow God to begin to do spiritual heart surgery on me. If we don't allow God to do spiritual heart surgery in us, we will never experience life the way we were created to live it. We will continue to see life and our circumstances through the tainted lenses we grew up with or the trauma we have endured even as adults. Sometimes our lenses become so cloudy, especially when we allow unforgiveness, bitterness, and hurt to fester. Walls get built around our heart, sometimes causing us to not trust God, not trust ourselves, and sometimes not even trust those who truly love us most.

I'll talk more about this a little later, but for now you need to know that as humans, *we* play a part in determining our future. Like I used to be, you may find yourself like a bird sitting in the cage with the door wide open. Despite freedom being right there for the taking, you have become so familiar with the cage that you just sit on your perch, not realizing the door is open for you and you actually have wings to soar. We can choose to stay caged within our prison walls of disappointment, unforgiveness, fear, etc., that surround our hearts, or we can choose to step into simple seed of trust and break free.

There is a price for true freedom. It looks like getting real, raw, and vulnerable. It looks like facing pain and can sometimes feel like a lonely road. It can be a long haul and downright frightening. It can be crazily frustrating, and feel really, really hard, but did you know that even pain can be a gift and an invitation from God? Yes, I said that! If I have learned anything in life, it is that:

Everything is an invitation into greater intimacy with the Father!

I promise you, you'll hear me say this more than once throughout this book; I can't say it enough! I understand pain and have navigated this road too many times to count. I also know that when we lean in and choose to pursue freedom, when we endure for a season, when we breakthrough, the joy *will* come. Like me, you can begin to step out into a place of mustard seed faith that will birth trust, enabling great growth and deep roots, building a sure foundation under you. Trust will lead you into greater faith, a faith that will truly move mountains and build legacy.

It's not easily obtained, and sometimes you have to be willing to step into the ring and fight for it. I understand the fight. Sometimes, in my young-adult life, it became a fight for life. There were times I wanted to end my life, and I had those thoughts and internal fights in my head and heart. Letting go and forgiving felt like I was losing if I did, like those who hurt me were winning. I didn't want to let go and trust God; it felt too scary. It felt hard. I didn't want to face the emotions of leaning in because it hurt so badly.

Growing up, I had heard many messages in church on forgiveness. As a church kid, I could practically repeat what someone was going to say when a message was preached on forgiveness. I knew the right things in my mind and in parts of my heart, but never saw true forgiveness modeled in my own family. I saw a lot of religion, gossip, backbiting, disappointment, and hypocrisy, centered around "forgiveness" by what was supposed to be loving family and loving church people. I learned early on not to trust people. I learned how to become a people pleaser in order to feel loved. I lived for the approval of man. I also learned how to keep people happy enough to "love me" or so I thought, but honestly, I kept them at a distance in my heart. I was a very compassionate person, yet, dysfunctional in my compassion. Did you know that compassion can become a dysfunction, causing you to not be real with people? Sometimes you can step into compassion out of a false sense of responsibility, or even people pleasing. The truth of the matter is, when you find yourself in situations like this, it is not reality and you don't have healthy boundaries. Maybe you think you do have healthy boundaries, but actually, you have walls instead of boundaries, and you can't have healthy boundaries if you've never *learned* to have them.

Did you know that compassion can become a dysfunction, causing you not to be real with people?

As a child, I was hurt over and over again by people who used me as a doormat. I also experienced the horrible childhood trauma of mental, physical, and sexual abuse, and because of that, at different points in my life I began to blame God. Mad at Him, I blamed Him for putting me in the family I was born into. I was so angry at Him because it felt like He didn't care or love us enough to provide for us financially. Lack of financial provision meant no extra things like going out to eat. In my mind, I thought the only way to experience "going out to eat" for a good hamburger was when I would find them and eat one out of the church trash can—sometimes after Sunday night church or even on Monday after the youth or nursery workers got their fill of Whataburger hamburgers on Sundays. Even if it was half eaten, I would eat it.

I hated the constant donated, hand-me-down clothes too (sometimes more like rags). I felt sorry for myself and my siblings. *Why are we 'that family' that can hardly afford new shoes, new clothes, never get a vacation, and many times don't know where our next meal is coming from?* I lived with a constant fear that we wouldn't have enough food to eat. Even into my adult years I often found myself waiting till everyone had eaten before I would eat.

Sometimes when you are so deeply wounded and hurt you learn to function in the dysfunction, but it is out of a place of pure survival, not thriving. It's so easy to want to hold the hurt inside, and for some people like me, you learn to stuff it down over the years. When this happens, the pain begins to give us a tainted view of who God really is, and it feels hard to partner with the small mustard seed of faith. The way we see God determines whether or not we feel we can trust Him enough, which in turn determines the measure of our faith we step into.

Do we see Him as good?

Do we see Him as loving?

Do we see Him as trustworthy?

In the trust is where we find faith to love again, to endure the storms of life, to forgive again, to believe for the impossible, and to dream again. If you are asking, "But how?" or "Mary, how do I get there?" The answer is simple: run at the lies! Ask yourself:

"What would it look like if Jesus had every part of my story, and I could finally trust and walk in a true relationship of trust and faith with Him?"

> What we *choose* to believe affects our behavior and everything in life, even our family legacy.

It is so important to run at the lies to tear them down and allow Jesus into every part of your life, and doing this takes mustard seed faith. The lies must be replaced with His truth. If you often find yourself with feelings or beliefs that He is not a good Father, that He will always disappoint and let you down, that He does not care about you, that He allowed that horrible thing to happen to you, then you, my friend, have built up walls keeping you from stepping into truth. If you don't go after the lies, you will always live with a false reality. What we *choose* to believe affects our behavior and everything in our life, even to the point of our family legacy.

What lies are you believing?

Here are a few of the major lies I have believed:

- **Some things never change.**

The truth is, with God, *all* things are possible (Matthew 19:36). So, it *is* possible to see breakthrough in all areas of your life and to see real change.

- **I am not good enough and will never amount to anything.**

The truth is, I am a new creation the moment I received Christ. The old man is gone!

Therefore, if anyone is in Christ, he is a new creation. The old has passed away; behold the new has come. —2 Corinthians 5:17

- **I'll never get out of debt; I was born into poverty, and that's just the way it is.**

The truth is, there is no lack in Heaven, and I have a rich Dad. Even the gates in Heaven are made with precious stones (Revelation 21:19–20). I can go to Him with anything, and when I ask for bread, He loves me so much as His daughter/son that He *won't* give me a stone (Matthew 7:9). He is so generous that even as I sleep, He gives to me. Psalm 127:2 says,

It is vain for you to rise early, to retire late, to eat the bread of anxious labors – For He gives to His beloved even in His sleep.

- **I'm not pretty enough.**

The truth is, I am made in the image of my Father, so therefore in Him I am perfect the way I am (Genesis 1:26). I am fearfully and wonderfully made (Psalm 139:14) by God, therefore there is no imperfection when I allow Him to have every part of me.

He loves us, and He is a generous Father. God wants to bring you into truth, even if it takes quieting your mind and heart while you sleep so He can accomplish His work in you. He will go as far as to minister to us, even in our sleep, so we can step into trust with our mustard seed faith. When God looks at you, He doesn't focus on what's wrong with you. He sees the amazing things, and He sees what is missing and what still needs work. The truth is, He loves us too much to leave us in that place. The missing things are only missing because of the lies we have chosen to partner with. In His kindness, He lovingly leads us into mustard seed trust which brings us into truth. His truth leads us into breakthrough so we're able to see that we *can* be whole again.

Have you ever felt like things were missing in you? I know I have, and part of that is because the enemy lies to us to keep us from God's truth about our lives. John 8:44 says the enemy is the father of lies. We know his goal is to keep us from truth, and when we choose to step in and unlock our small seed of faith, we begin to realize there is always room for deeper healing and greater growth. Why? Because there is always more available to us in the Kingdom of God. In 2 Corinthians 3:18, the Bible tells us that He will take us *from glory to glory*. In God's loving kindness, He always draws us into greater greatness, and sometimes that means letting go.

Are there things in your life that you believe that hinder you from stepping into your greatness and your destiny?

Friend, it's time to let them go!

Chapter 2

Letting Go For A Greater Future

When I think about letting go, my mind immediately goes to a picture of a little girl holding a helium balloon, releasing it, and watching it fly up, up, up, and away. Eventually, the balloon becomes a miniature dot in the sky until she can no longer see it. It takes patience to watch it get to that point, but somehow, when she can no longer see it, she feels a sweet satisfaction. Why? Her patience has paid off. As a girl, I loved watching helium balloons rise into the sky and was mesmerized by them, and even as an adult I still love to release them and watch them float up and away.

Having four children, we have a lot of helium balloons pass through our home, especially during our March through June birthday season which is three months of lots of helium balloons! When those balloons start losing their air after a couple weeks, sometimes that little girl inside of me still loves to go outside and release them. Even when there isn't much air in it, a helium balloon still flies up, up, up, and away, rather high, until it becomes a speck. If you and I were standing there together, you'd see me smile and probably sigh as I watched it go. *Ahhh, sweet satisfaction...*

Forgiveness is a lot like the imagery of a helium balloon. We have to be willing to hold it, look at it, and let it go. When we let it go, it's not like magic; it won't disappear suddenly. There is no mystical, euphoric exchange that happens like when Elsa from *Frozen* sings her song! It can take some time before we feel unforgiveness tangibly loosen its grip on us, but like that balloon, it fades over time like a distant memory. You will feel the ache and pain sometimes, and some days will be easier than others. Forgiveness can sometimes be like holding a balloon before our Heavenly Father daily and choosing to let it go again and again.

Forgiveness is a major key to unlocking mustard seed faith, and without it, we have a hard time trusting and believing that it's going to be okay to let go. When we do let go, release forgiveness, and choose to trust God, His peace that surpasses all understanding, no matter the circumstance or situation, covers us. You may be thinking, *You have no idea what I've been through! How can I really let go and forgive?* Trust me, I've been through many difficult battles which felt like hell and back in my life. I have walked long, hard roads and have years of experience in choosing to let go and to allow my forgiveness balloon to be released.

As a little girl and teen, I was hurting, mad, broken, and lonely. My heart ached. There were many nights of crying myself to sleep when nobody was around. Vivid memories still swirl of hot tears rolling down my cheeks, wetting my hair, and my pillow being soaked with tears. I can remember the long days and nights, because I wanted to be mad at God for allowing me to be *born into this family. This is not fair, God!*

You see, as a child, I was sexually abused in horrible ways. I won't go into detail, but in the future, I may write about that journey in another book. Just know I've been there, and I truly have a real understanding of feelings that scream, *HOW CAN I LET GO? HOW CAN I TRULY FORGIVE?* The thoughts I had of ending it all were very real because I genuinely felt nobody cared about my life. Thank God I never could, and thankfully those thoughts never became a reality.

God, in His kindness, never lets us stay in a place of unforgiveness or anger when we lean into Him. He is a King, yet a gentle, loving Father full of grace and mercy. Just like it says in Luke 15:3–7, He truly does leave the 99 to come after the one. He came after me one day when I was in worship. In college, I knew the Lord and loved the Lord, yet a place of unforgiveness in my heart toward Him and others lingered. In that moment, standing there while the worship band was singing, I had what was like an open-eyed vision. It played out like a movie, and I saw myself in a full stadium on the stage, ministering alongside others. It was the end of the service, and we were praying for people. The stage was located in the center of what seemed like a football field and everyone ministering had lines of people in front of us waiting to be prayed for. I was on the edge of the stage, laying hands on people's heads one after the other as they walked up to the edge of the stage for prayer and an impartation. All of a sudden in front of me was my stepfather, who was a minister when I was a child, yet, he was also my abuser. He was like the devil in disguise. In reality, he was the preacher in the pulpit on some Sundays, but he was like the devil in our house when he was home Monday through Saturday. Back to the vision, in that moment as I saw it was my stepfather in front of me wanting prayer, I audibly heard God ask me,

> God is a King, yet a gentle loving Father full of grace and mercy.

"Mary, will you choose to forgive?"

Suddenly, the vision changed and transitioned to this very real scene of the cross and the crucifixion. I saw Jesus being stabbed, brutally beaten, and tortured. I saw the horrible gushes of blood, I saw the water pouring out of His side, I saw the crown of thorns being pushed into His skull—to the point where His face was no longer recognizable. It was horrific, and I started ugly crying—if you know what I mean. It's the kind of crying where lots of tissues are required, uncontrollable sobbing, snot running out of your nose for the whole world to see, big, swollen eyes from the many tears, and mascara is smeared all down your face. Thank God for waterproof mascara now! But yup, in that moment, that was me. It was very intense, and I could hardly watch as my heart swelled with pain. I could physically feel torturous pain inside of my heart as this was happening. Then, I heard God the Father say this to me:

"How can you not forgive him, Mary, when I forgave the ones who did this to My Son?"

I knew God was inviting me into a sacred place of laying things down and choosing real forgiveness. It didn't feel hard in that moment, it felt sweet, raw, and tender. That day, I chose forgiveness. I saw a picture of my stepfather Bob, my abuser, in that open-eyed, movie-like vision, and I chose to look in his face and say, "I forgive you!" That day, my balloon floated up, up, up, and away, and I never looked back. Was it all roses after that? No! It wasn't.

However, after that day, I never again dealt with the raging bitterness and anger inside that was wrapped up in unforgiveness. Daily, I would choose to let Father God take it. I exchanged my balloon of unforgiveness for greater peace of mind and heart. As I said, things were not all roses though after this because I realized later that

I had unforgiveness toward God. I was still mad at Him and had to repent.

Another realization hit me like a ton of bricks too. I realized I had never had the chance to really be a child and found myself in a season of mourning the loss of my childhood in the weeks, months, and year following the encounter. Later, other things started coming up, like unforgiveness toward my biological father who was never in my life and never there for me. I also had unforgiveness toward my mother who I felt was never there for me as a child.

She was a single mom who took care of us the best she knew how. Now as an adult looking back, I can see and know that she also suffered from pain from her own childhood. Her unhealed pain filtered into a lack of love and not showing up as a healthy parent. I don't remember being hugged often, and I chose to forgive her for not really showing me love in that way. I also chose to forgive her for never really pouring into me the way I thought a good mother should, and I chose to forgive her for not protecting me from my stepfather the way I felt she should have.

The raw reality was, she often emotionally and physically was absent throughout my childhood. It hurt, I was mad, and in my journey, I chose to forgive. The path to forgiveness felt like it was a long road; however, in the end, it was the love of Jesus that helped me. Because of Him and through His loving kindness I realized I could release forgiveness and be free from the bondage of pain and lack of trust that had held me captive for so long. I realized I could be free from my prison of pain, from the ones who had deeply wounded me, but it was *my* choice.

There really is no greater gift you can offer God than your heart, especially when there is deep pain and deep wounding from the very people supposed to protect you. Forgiveness and letting go are a beautiful sacrifice to the Lord. A heart that understands, that chooses to believe in the power of forgiveness, and chooses to release that balloon is a beautiful aroma to God and to others.

Many times we choose to stay in this mental place of unforgiveness because somehow we believe it protects us. Or in a weird way, we think it's punishing the ones who hurt us. The truth of the matter is, it's a lie we are choosing to believe. Our abusers are not held in a prison by our unforgiveness. They still live their lives daily all around us, yet we are the ones holding *ourselves* captive by creating an internal prison. We think we are holding them in it, but in reality, *we* are in this prison.

Some of you reading this know *exactly* what I'm talking about. You get it, and you know it's time to let go! I'm not saying it will be easy. Forgiving feels difficult for many of us because we want justice, and letting go, especially when we're at the beginning of this journey, feels so unjust. It feels like we lose, but in reality, we win.

I have a high justice meter. People like me who have a high justice meter want justice or revenge for the offenses we and others have suffered. Some of you feel like I used to feel. You feel that if you forgive and let go, then there's no justice. If you are like I was, you have ongoing conversations and questions in your head like, *Why should I let them off the hook?* But they *aren't* off the hook. It really is between each individual person and God. God has their number. He will deal with them fairly, which is something we cannot do in and of ourselves.

The Bible says in Psalm 33:5 that He loves justice. In 2 Thessalonians 1:6–8 it says God is just, and He will pay back those who afflict or wrong you. Matthew 18:6 says that whoever causes a little one who believes in Him to stumble, it would be better for him to have a heavy millstone hung around his neck and to be drowned in the depth of the sea.

There will be a payback time! I always tell my children that when they make bad choices, there are always consequences to their actions. The ones who have hurt or abused you, mark my words, they will NOT be off the hook. "Justice is mine," says the Lord (Romans 12:19). There are always consequences to a person's actions. God is a God of justice, and yet He still requires us to forgive. It's like He is saying,

"Let go my beloved, don't hold onto these things because I've got this. I want you to be free so I can hold your heart and show you what healthy relationship really looks like! I want you to be free so you can truly experience the joy of truly living."

Jesus makes it plain; we know where He stands when it comes to forgiveness in His Word. We are called to extend and show forgiveness no matter what. I believe there is a great reward in letting things like unforgiveness go and letting God into those hard places, especially when it is the most difficult to release.

In Matthew 18:21–22, one of Jesus' disciples (Peter) asks Jesus a question. He asks,

"Lord, how often shall my brother sin against me and I forgive him? Up to seven times?" Jesus said to him "I do not say to you, up to seven times, but up to seventy times seven!"

In Colossians 3:13, the Apostle Paul, inspired by the Holy Spirit, instructs us to,

Make allowance for each other's faults, and forgive anyone who offends you. Remember, the Lord forgave you, so you must forgive others.

You may be thinking, *I can never forgive (__________)* (insert the person's name), or you just simply feel like you can never let go. I want to tell you that your feelings are valid, but our feelings don't always tell the truth. The truth is, you can forgive! You can let go! It's up to you whether or not you want to rise up and choose to be powerful and do it.

What we really mean when we say we can't forgive is *I don't want to forgive them. They deserve to suffer or hurt the same way they caused me to.* I would ask you, do they really? As I've gotten older, one thing I have realized is hurting people hurt people, so do they really deserve to suffer? What they need is healing just like you and me. If it were impossible to forgive, God wouldn't have commanded us to. He wouldn't have suffered the torture of the cross on our behalf.

If you are reading this book and your heart is beating fast right now, I know this chapter is for you. If you are like how I used to be, and you find it hard to trust and walk in faith because of past abuse in your life, I am so sorry you were subjected to that. I so get it! Whatever happened to you, whatever was said, whatever wrongs were done against you, it is NOT okay! I'm sorry that someone took advantage of you and hurt you. I'm sorry that someone didn't really see you and walked all over you. I'm sorry about the leader in church who hurt you. I'm sorry that parent wasn't emotionally there for you or was absent in your life, or that they walked out on, abandoned, or abused you. I'm sorry that a mom or dad was never

> If it were impossible to forgive, God wouldn't have commanded us to forgive.

there for you. I'm sorry that a sister, a brother, a best friend, or a spouse walked out on you or hurt you deeply.

God knows your pain. He sees the walls. He sees the walls of "protection" you have built around your heart. Like I said, they are not walls of protection; they are prison walls that the enemy wants to control you with. These walls are what the enemy has helped you to create to keep you in your pain and prison. He never wants you to walk in true freedom. These walls keep roots of unforgiveness, bitterness, hate, and shame deep inside you. Sometimes these walls even manifest in our lives in physical health issues. Like an ugly cancer, they keep growing deeper and deeper roots, day after day, week after week, month after month, year after year, chipping away at your heart until finally they eat you alive.

Things like unforgiveness, bitterness, anger, etc., are invisible chains that imprison us on the inside and create road blocks to our relationship with God. They keep us from truly feeling Him, from truly hearing Him, from truly trusting Him, from fully walking with Him and from *fully* having faith in Him. It's time to be free, but freedom is a choice.

Let me yell this over you: YOU ARE POWERFUL! Yes, you are powerful to make that wise decision and choose to be free. But the question is, how bad do you want it? If you want to experience freedom from the chains that bind and hinder you from trusting and walking in faith in a good, good Father, you really have to choose to release some things. You have to *choose* to let go and forgive. It's time to confess from your mouth, and forgive from your heart.

You might be wondering, *How do I do this? How do I forgive from the heart?* I get it, because I have been there. Forgiveness for me was a choice, and I had to choose to first acknowledge the pain, acknowledge the unforgiveness, acknowledge the hate I had toward the other person(s). I had to find the open door, the root of where the offense started, where the pain first entered into my heart. I sat with the Lord and began to open my heart to Him. I chose to trust Him and allow Him into my heart. I wanted the roots of unforgiveness, bitterness, and anger gone.

If you don't deal with the root and close that door, then you will never allow true forgiveness and freedom to manifest. Sit with God, tell Him you are choosing to be brave, and trust Him in that space. Allow Him to bring all the pain and all the hurt to the surface so He can deal with it. This is where healing really begins. This is where the chains that bind you begin to lose their grip. This is where freedom begins to manifest in your body, spirit, and soul.

I want to encourage you to stop what you're doing right now. When I went after this in my own life, I had to quiet my heart, and I encourage you to quiet yours too. Find a space where you can just quiet your heart and mind. In the following pages there is space for you to write down what the Holy Spirit is speaking to you and showing you. If you think you might need more space, get more paper and sit with the Holy Spirit. Ask Him to bring to mind anything that's hindering your relationship with Him and anyone you need to forgive. If you deal with anger or bitterness, ask Him where the open door to it first happened in your life. Don't overthink it. Usually, it's what you hear or picture in your mind first.

As you listen with your heart, take your paper, write down what you hear, and begin to make a list. This list could include a parent(s), grandparent(s), boyfriend(s), girlfriend(s), brother(s), sister(s), pastor(s), boss(es), son(s), daughter(s), and even yourself. The reality is, most of us are harder on ourselves than anyone else ever would be. I know I have been in the past. So, if you need to forgive yourself, do it.

It's time to forgive yourself and whoever the Holy Spirit brings to mind. Take back the ground the enemy has stolen in your life! You may find that instances or people you've blocked from your memory come up. Don't be afraid to go there. If God brings it to your mind, allow the Holy Spirit to lead you into freedom. God, in His kindness, will leave no stone unturned if you give Him space to really navigate this heart journey with you. If the Lord brings a name or face to your mind and you don't know why, write it down anyway even if it feels insignificant. It could carry more weight than you understand in the spirit realm. This journey with your heart won't always be easy. Sometimes it may hurt and feel like hell, but I encourage you to not give up. In His faithfulness and kindness, as a good and loving Heavenly Father, He will walk with you. He's got you and will hold you as you navigate this heart journey together.

First, let's use the space below to write down the thoughts and feelings the Lord highlights and the people He's asking you to forgive. Once you've done this, I will then lead you through some inner-healing prayers to read aloud. With each prayer, I've created space alongside it for you to write down what the Father speaks to you. I have also created a playlist of instrumental music for you to have playing in the background if you want as you do this, which you can access by scanning this QR code.

Deep Dive Into Repentance Prayer:

Heavenly Father,
I choose to step into mustard seed faith today.
I choose to believe that You are kind, You are full of grace, and that You are full of mercy and patience, especially with me.
I choose to believe that it's Your kindness that leads me to repentance (Romans 2:4). *And so today, I choose to draw near to You, knowing You love me and that You are right here with me.*

I ask You to wash my heart clean.
I know I haven't always walked in forgiveness, and at times I have chosen bitterness and have built walls around my heart, that have kept me from You and from people who care.
Please forgive me for not extending forgiveness toward others who have hurt me, offended me, stolen from me, wronged me, abused me physically, mentally, or emotionally, etc..
Instead, I have held onto anger, bitterness, hatred, and resentment for (__________) in my heart.

(Write down whatever applies to you here in the blank space, then say it and confess it.)

____

____

____

____

____

____

____

____

Holy Spirit, I ask You right now to bring to my mind all the people I need to forgive so that I may be truly free to trust You fully and have unmovable, unshakable, big faith in You (Matthew 18:35).

Heart Healing Exercise 1

If you only wrote what you're feeling and or hearing and didn't already do this, I want you to be brave and begin to write down the names that come to mind, then continue the prayer. If this isn't enough space for you, get another piece of paper.

Father, in the name of Jesus Christ of Nazareth who came in the flesh, and in obedience and trust in You, I choose to forgive the following people:

____

____

____

____

____

____

____

____

____

____

____

____

____

____

(Now, go through the list you made above one by one, with as many names as it takes as shown in the example below.)

I choose to forgive and release (person's name) *for...* (describe what he/she did).

If you have a hard time thinking of names of people, but you know that you have unforgiveness in your heart or you have anger, bitterness, self-hatred, etc., ask Holy Spirit to show you where the open door (the point of entry) is. Find out where these things first came in. Sometimes God will speak it to you in your heart, or you may see a picture. However He chooses to reveal it doesn't matter; what matters is that you activate your little mustard seed of faith, step into trust, step out into obedience, and cut ties with whatever He reveals to you. Close the door on it so that it will no longer have a hold in you and over you.

Heart Healing Exercise 2

After writing down what He shows or speaks to you, continue the prayer.

Father, thank you for showing me where this (_______) first came in.

(Fill in the blank and name the thing—unforgiveness/bitterness/self-hatred, etc.)

I speak to this spirit of (__________) (fill in the blank with all the things that apply—anger, bitterness, self-hatred, depression, poverty) *and I refuse to partner with you anymore.*
I cast you out and send you back to where you came from, and I close the door to you in my life forever, in the name of Jesus Christ of Nazareth!

Encouragement

God always loves to give good gifts to His children, so after closing the door to these things, there is a sweet exchange that can take place. I would encourage you to ask Jesus to show you what gift(s) He wants to give you by continuing the prayer below.

Gift Prayer

Jesus, I know You are proud of me. Thank you for helping me to get rid of (____________) (fill in the blank). *I know You love to give good gifts to Your children, so, Jesus, in place of (____________)* (what you just closed the door on) *what gift would You like to give me?* (Write down below what you hear or see.)

Now, listen with your heart. Sometimes He will speak "My peace," or "My freedom," or "Joy." I have done this, my husband and kids have done this, and so have the countless others I've led through inner healing. Sometimes we get pictures of something, and sometimes it may be a word(s) that He speaks. Whatever He tells you, write it and own it!

____

____

____

____

____

____

____

____

Prayer Of Ownership

Father God,
Thank you for helping me break down the walls around my heart.
Thank you for helping me close the doors that should not be open
and for setting me free from the bondage of (________________) (fill in the blank) *and everything that's been holding me back from You.*
Thank you, Jesus, that You are good and that You love to give Your children good gifts. In place of (____________) (fill in the blank), *You have given me a gift of (__________)* (fill in the blank). *I am choosing to let go and I receive Your gift to me.*

In some cases, if you are like me, it wasn't an overnight thing. So, it's important to use the "I choose to forgive and release" phrase in everyday life when you feel it's needed. Doing this ensures no door is left cracked open for the enemy to set up camp in any way, fashion, or form, because if you even give him an inch, he will try to take a foothold. It's important to take notice when the enemy tries to bring back accusations to those things you shut the door on. If you need to follow it up daily by thanking God for setting you free from the bondage of anger, bitterness, hatred, unforgiveness, shame, etc., do it! If you don't feel like it, remember our feelings lie to us sometimes.

You may not feel the freedom right away, but you eventually will as you continue to choose to step into it. Step into thankfulness and praise for what is happening. Thankfulness is a key into greater freedom. You may have to say it several times in one day—for weeks or even months. Do this until you no longer feel the negativity of the thing that has festered in your heart. If you wake up one day, finding yourself thinking about the offense, and it stirs a familiar or negative emotion in your heart, go through the prayers again. As you do this, you will begin to realize that it really does work!

There is power in JESUS and power in our words. As we step into mustard seed faith, that faith begins to change the way we think and perceive things. It also begins to grow powerfully strong roots in a godly foundation. Your words have the power to create a space for God to heal you, and through that healing, His love will begin to fill you and manifest in and through you. Soon you will wake up and realize, *Oh my goodness, I don't think like that anymore. I don't have that fear anymore,* or *the pain is gone, I'm not numb, and I can feel Him again.* Hallelujah!

Love is *key*—so very important to our everyday life, both physically and mentally. When God's love flows in you, it creates an atmosphere where faith arises, and you step into true trust. Our ability as believers in Christ to walk in love toward ourselves and one another creates an atmosphere for God (who is Love) to manifest Himself among us by His Spirit—the Holy Spirit. The gifts of the Holy Spirit are manifested in us and through us when we allow His love to fully permeate every area of our minds and hearts. Romans 12:2 says to be transformed by the renewing of your mind. This is what having a renewed mind is all about, and this is what will unlock mustard seed faith to trust and to step into greater faith.

If you have taken the time to do this, I am so proud of you! If you got through this chapter and sat with the Holy Spirit and journeyed that road of forgiveness, well done for leaning in! I know it most likely wasn't easy, but I promise it will be worth it. There is nothing like living in true freedom with the Father. The more you lean into Him, the more your lenses of life will change, and you will begin to see life differently as you let love take root in every area of your heart.

Chapter 3

The Lenses Of Your Life

Have you ever thought about the lenses you see life through? We all have lenses shaped by our life experiences, the way we were raised, what we were exposed to, what we expose ourselves to, hardships we've experienced, and more. More often than not, we aren't even aware of them. We often interpret God, the Bible, and life through the lenses we grow up with and those of our life experiences. The way we see God and the way we choose to show up in life will determine the shape of our future.

One of my greatest struggles has been having enough faith to trust that God is a good Provider. Growing up in poverty was no joke. It causes a person to see things through the lenses of lack. I grew up without a father and was raised in a poor, single-parent home. I was always told, "We don't have enough money." We couldn't go camping because *we don't have enough money*. We can't have a birthday party because *we don't have enough money*. Sorry, no sports because *we don't have enough money*. You can't have that hamburger because *we don't have enough money*.

For the record, I absolutely love hamburgers now because of the *can'ts* I endured! It seemed like my household's mantra was "NO." My dreams felt like they were always squashed because of the poverty spirit that blinded my family's eyes. It caused them to see through poverty lenses, and in turn, shaped the mentality of *there is just never enough* in my own life.

Remember the awful phrase *money doesn't grow on trees*? My mother and others around me would say this so often. I can hear some of you laughing, because you know exactly what I'm talking about, or maybe you're a parent and you've said that to your children. I refuse to say it because I learned later in life that the phrase is a lie. Money can grow on trees! The truth is, there are so many products that create wealth from raw materials that we have access to and use in our world today. Think about orchards and other farms. It's like money does grow on their trees, right?

Besides, it's a phrase rooted in poverty thinking and encourages a poverty way of thinking when spoken over people. Please don't ever repeat the lie I grew up with over your children because I believe, as I said, it's a lie! I believe it's a lie from satan that helps seed the spirit of poverty over young, impressionable hearts.

Let's take a look at trees themselves and the wood we use from them. There are so many products made from wood: pencils, paper, houses, chicken coops, barns, furniture, toothpicks, baseball bats, musical instruments, drumsticks, handles, charcoal, toys, some bow ties (yes, I've seen wooden bow ties with my own eyes), fences, floors, boats, bridges, cabinets, canes, boxes, coffins, barrels, decks, docks, doors, matches, canoes and paddles, picture frames, window frames, bed frames, school rulers, and on and on. So, yes, money grows on trees. In reality, it's all about our perspective. It's all about the lenses we have, and how we see things. You can just see the tree taking up space, maybe providing shade, or you can see the bigger picture.

Now that I'm an adult, in some ways I totally understand the *no* over many wants and desires in my young life. Raised by a single mother, on a single income that never paid much, she had six of us kids to take care of. My mother struggled *a lot,* and I remember her being stressed about bills, gas money, rent, etc. The financial pressure was real. Thankfully, my grandparents (who I absolutely adored, especially my Grandmother Mitsu) were close by, and although they couldn't give us money—as they, too, struggled with lack—they helped watch us kids. This helped my mother to not have a large monthly childcare bill. More often than not, I can remember spending many days with my grandparents because my mother was working or just out, so there wasn't much time for anything else, and there was never enough money to do lots of fun things. We did get to do some fun things like going to the Cherry Blossom festival in San Francisco and getting to eat green tea ice cream. However, fun memories were few and far between.

Throwing off those lenses of lack and poverty when it's all you've known is a real battle, but with God, it *is* possible. In His kindness, He allows the Holy Spirit to lead and guide us into all truth when we choose Him and seek Him. The truth is, with Him we *are* able. Even though poverty always knocked on the door of our belief systems, some of my sisters, against all odds, dared to believe God. They stepped into their mustard seed of faith enough to push past this type of thinking in some areas of their lives. They chose to let go and throw off the lenses of poverty that would try to blind them from truth, and I have watched them go after their dreams. Two of them were single mothers when they stepped out to pursue their dreams.

I was so proud when my oldest sister Elaisa broke through one area of the poverty mentality of *not enough* and put herself through college. She was the first college graduate in our immediate family—out of us six siblings. She later went back to school for her masters and became a special-needs teacher. It was because of her that I felt I could do college as well, and she, in some ways, set the standard for me when it came to finishing college.

I am proud of my brother Daniel who has worked his butt off at the same job for years and has consistently been there as a loving father to his kids, even when he had no example of what a good, loving father should be like. In my eyes, that's a huge accomplishment considering all we went through as kids. Today's statistics show that kids who grow up without a father are more likely to not be present fathers themselves. It takes a real man to show up for his kids and be a father.

I was also so proud when one of my younger sisters, Ruth, bought her first home as a single mother. She had fear—to a degree—yet stood in faith and broke through the barrier of *not enough money*. In the face of fear, she chose to trust, allowing God to show her a way to step out and do it. She found God faithful in the process.

Just as I was proud of Ruth, I was also so proud when I watched my youngest baby sister, Rebecca, as a single mother, step out and do something she had always been intimidated to do: pursue a martial arts dream. She started finding her voice through it and moved on to do competitive Brazilian Jiu Jitsu. She began to pursue different belts and moved up the ranks, and in the process, she overcame her own fears. At the writing of this book, she teaches women's self-defense classes, and she is now a black belt. She also has a dream to potentially own her own clothing line, and perhaps one day she will. She also has authored a book called *Daily Declarations* and is in the process of releasing a second book. She is such a go getter and runs at her Goliaths. She has a dream to write more and isn't afraid to step out to achieve it. Stepping into her dreams brought her into a realm of confidence that she is growing in, and in this space, she is compelled to share her story of trauma and breakthrough with others and lead women and men into their own journey of healing.

There comes a time when you no longer take *no* for an answer. As you do that, your lenses begin to change, you break the barrier, and you step into trust through a mustard seed of faith. Now that I'm an adult and a mother to four precious children, I can understand in the natural realm the different financial seasons. In some, it seems there just isn't enough, especially when bills pile up and your dreams grow seemingly further and further away. Even in the midst of those times, I have grown to also understand that when you see through the lenses of our Heavenly Father, the mustard seed of faith is real. You can take that seed, nurture it, and water it until you step into trust, and this is when the lie of *never enough* begins to fade. Shackles loosen from your mind, and the poverty way of thinking becomes no more when you realize the truth: *there is always enough in the Kingdom of God.* His Kingdom never has any lack.

I have an old, torn-up 365 daily devotional titled *Smith Wigglesworth Devotional* that I've had for years. I love it so much and use it daily. Smith was a man of great faith, known as a "Healing Evangelist." He saw incredible healings and countless people get healed, delivered, saved, and set free from demonic oppression. As I spent time with God recently and read in my devotional, this line jumped off the page:

"God rejoices when we manifest a faith that holds God to His word."

WOW...yes! Imagine the Father jumping up and down, rejoicing in the throne room, watching us take hold of that mustard seed of faith and hold steadfast to His truth. There He is, watching you, in your pain, in your uncertainty, listening to your heart as He hears you saying, "*God, You are good*! God, there is no lack in Your Kingdom! God, You are faithful! God, You say in Your Word when I, Your child, ask for bread, God, You won't give me a stone! Father, I choose to trust You!"

God rejoices when we manifest a faith that holds Him to His Word.

When we choose to take hold of Him and step into His truth like this, I know He is like a proud Papa over us as His children. I have heard this said several times by a pastor of Zion Christian Fellowship in Powell Ohio named Jim Baker:

"Nobody can take better care of me than Dad!"

I love this phrase, because as I grow and lean into Him, I realize He's not a distant God; He is my Dad, He is my Papa. He is Abba who loves to take care of His kids, and He is *so* good. He knows our desires, even if they're as simple and as small as a purple Walkman!

Your faith will only explore the level of goodness that you see God having, only when you choose to lean in and build relationship with Him. When your view of Him is distorted, you'll look at Him through the lenses of mistrust, brokenness, betrayal, and lack. You will feel that He is only good sometimes or that He will come through for others but maybe not fully for you. God desires relationship, and in that relationship, total abandonment to Him. You will never abandon yourself to someone you don't believe you can trust or who isn't good. Stepping into this didn't feel easy for me, especially once I realized I had carried this mentality for so long. I carried it all the way into my adulthood because of the distorted lenses I saw life through. It wasn't until I had kids when I began to understand that it really was a spirit over my mindset and heart that was choking out certain areas of freedom, especially financial freedom. It clouded my vision to truly see God as a good and faithful Provider and Father.

> You will never abandon yourself to someone you don't believe you can trust.

Later, I realized I could choose to partner with this negative way of thinking, or I could choose to stand in faith and believe God. I could *choose* to believe that I will always be in lack. After all, past circumstances seemed to "prove" that. Or instead, I could *choose* to partner with Heaven and believe there is no lack in the Kingdom of God and that my Father loves to give good gifts to His children. He loves to provide for me, not because of how good I am or what I can do for Him, but simply because I am the King's kid. I am His daughter, I have all access to His Kingdom, His Kingdom lives in me and through me, and He delights in me. I realized it's not about how good I am or how much I could pray and declare His Word. Although those things are great, it was simply learning instead to take that mustard seed faith of trust, to fall in love with Him, and learn to rest in Him and His goodness over me, and out of that, my lenses changed.

Again, I want to emphasize how this process takes time and doesn't always happen overnight. By making a daily choice to trust God with your mustard seed of faith, your relationship with Him grows stronger and stronger until, before you know it, you begin to notice a powerful root system that runs deep and wide. It has created a massive tree of unshakable faith, built on a foundation of trust, that all sprouted from a tiny mustard seed of faith.

All these years later, I still know I *can* trust God—not just in small ways, but in big ways too. He is good, and trusting Him is easy. I can stand in faith, be obedient, and be a good steward of what I do have, and when I've done all I can do, I simply stand. In that place, I can rest in His secure arms as a daughter with a big, powerful, wonderful Kingly Dad.

Rest is huge, yet many people don't find it necessary to choose it. Often, when your eyes are veiled and you look at life through the lenses of pain, frustration, lack, poverty, and other negativity, it's hard to see rest. Therefore, it feels hard to find it and step into it. When bills were due and I saw no money coming in, I couldn't find my floor of faith...and I for sure wasn't resting. I instantly turned to the spirit of control while thinking, *Hmmm, what monies can I maneuver around?* as if money was like a chess piece on a board to be played with. I would also try and manipulate which bills I could pay later, even if they were already late to begin with. Come on, let' get real...some of you totally know what I'm talking about.

My heart was more often than not filled with anxiety and fear. I found myself thinking, *What if God doesn't come through?* There have been too many times to count when I would turn to my husband Peter with fear in my eyes and say, "What are we going to do?" He would in turn, remind me, "We are going to pray and trust God!" Thank God for husbands who are steady pillars of strength to lean on.

Sixteen years of my life were spent on the mission field in Africa, and I took on the false responsibility of feeling like I was supposed to be this incredible person of great faith. I was, after all, a missionary who had been rebirthed in the fires of the Brownsville Revival, known as the "Pensacola Outpouring," yet I was terrified inside when I saw lack staring me down. I would revert back to the worried little girl who saw God as a stingy tyrant, ruling over me with an iron fist. Jumping through performance hoops, I felt like I had to do everything right—tithe more, give more, pray more, read my Bible more, do more. Subconsciously, I truly believed if I checked all the right boxes (again, performance), only then would He provide for me. More often than not, I saw God as someone who would provide for others but not for me, which I'm sure some of you reading this can relate to. I viewed situations like this through the lens of poverty, and that poverty lens is rooted in an orphan spirit. I served Him without even realizing I was trying to earn His favor and love through my works, rather than out of a pure love and devotion to Him, simply as His beloved daughter.

My trust levels were low. I had always thought of myself as a person with big faith, and I was when it came to others or mission projects, but when it came to my needs and trusting God for *me*, my faith levels were so low. Inwardly, when it came down to the truth of it, I questioned whether I was really worthy. I didn't know or understand my true worth simply as a daughter, and I didn't know how to trust Him for me, for my needs, and the needs of my family. *How do I simply be His daughter and rest in Him, knowing He is a good Father?* I wasn't sure.

In 2019 I hit burn out, and God began to work on my heart. That's when I began to realize it's about coming into sonship and rest inside of yourself more than anything else, and this leads to simple, easy devotion. Yes, it really is easy! It's about finding His peace in your heart and saying,

"God, I choose to trust You! I give You, my bills. I give this lack to You. You say You are good, and I know You are. I trust You. Now, what are You going to do about this, and how do You want me to partner with You in this?"

Right now, as I write these words, tears are welling up in my eyes. God is moving my heart as I'm sitting in a coffee shop. I look up from my computer, and outside, through the big picture window in front of me, I see a father on the sidewalk with his daughter who can't be more than 11 or 12 months old. I can tell she just learned to walk as she is a bit unsteady, not totally sure of herself yet. Her father bends down to her level, looks her in the eyes, holds his arms out and assures her by saying, "Trust me, Daddy's here. Just come. I've got you!" That, my friend, is the simplicity of the Father. This is how good He is. He comes down, meets us eye to eye, He holds His arms out, and says, "Come, baby girl, come, baby boy...trust Me. Daddy's here, just come. I've got you!"

Do we trust Him enough to just come to Him, even if we are a bit unsteady, even if we have lost our balance, even if we're a little messy, even if we have lost our way and lost our focus? Will we simply trust Him and come? Will we say, "God, here I am, every bit of me. Here I AM!"

Coming to the Father means vulnerability, and many of us, if we are honest, run from vulnerability. We run from laying our hearts bare. Sometimes it's pride that keeps us in the same place, sometimes it's the false need to keep up a certain image, sometimes it's fear of feeling like a failure, sometimes fear of rejection or not being accepted. Maybe it's fear of commitment or fear of being faced with truth. But many, many times it's really just *shame.* Maybe shame that we don't actually know how to manage ourselves or how to manage our money, and we've made a mess of it. Sometimes it's the shame of choosing our own way instead of partnering with Him and choosing the path He has for us. Sometimes it's the shame we feel about the consequences of our choices that are noticeable to us and everyone else, and we just want to run away and hide.

But the truth is, many times we don't have it all together and we need help. Many times, we know we've hit a wall and feel like we have nowhere to turn. Life can feel hard in different seasons. Money can be tight at times. But I know that as a parent in those challenging seasons and situations, my heart is always to give my kids their hearts' desires, and that is our Heavenly Father's heart for us too. When something feels too far out of reach for us financially, I choose to trust God, partnering in faith, believing that He will make a way. I choose to stop and ask Him, "God, what do you want us to do? What do I carry in my hands currently that can create some wealth right now?" God always makes a way when you're willing to step out with Him.

There was one year when Thanksgiving and Christmas were right around the corner, but we had loads of bills due and Christmas presents to buy and absolutely no money. Now, I have always been the kind of person to buy gifts here and there throughout the year when I see things on sale, and it helps. I love getting the shopping done early, and most years I manage that well. We have a goal to make Christmas awesome and to buy nice, fun gifts for our kids without going broke or into debt doing it. We don't usually buy extravagantly; however, we have always tried to buy them at least one big present—something their heart really desires. The thrill of buying gifts and hiding them until Christmas has always been fun, but it's so darn hard to hide them all!

During this particular holiday season, our bank account was completely empty. We were broke students in ministry school, and we had been on a journey with God, learning a lot about stewarding our finances well with Kingdom thinking and trusting God. Looking back, I know we were in a faith bootcamp. In this season, there were several things we learned that stuck out to us. *Thankfulness* was the first thing—a major key to breakthrough.

In Matthew 14:13–21, when Jesus took the five loaves and two fish, the very first thing He did was raise them up to Heaven, then He looked up, and He *thanked the Father*. So, being reminded of what Jesus did, that is what we began to do. If we found a penny on the ground, got a check in the mail, or had cash given to us, we started pulling our family together like in a team huddle, and we would lay our hands on the money and yell, "Thank you, Jesus!" Peter and I would pray out loud that God would multiply it. He would *always* multiply it as we stepped out in faith.

Stepping out and *meeting God half way* was the second key to breakthrough we were learning. Like the story of Elijah and the widow in 1 Kings 17:8–24, she was going to use the last bit of flour and oil she had to make a little bread for her and her son, and then, in her words, *just die.* She was partnering with the war in the second Heaven over her provision, and she was looking at her circumstances through the lenses of the natural realm. She was ready to throw in the towel.

When Elijah the Prophet came to her, she took what little mustard seed faith she had, chose to believe the word of the Lord, stepped into trust, partnered with Heaven, and stepped out, borrowing jars for oil from all her neighbors. With that little mustard seed of faith, she began to fill the jars with what little oil she had. Wow, what happened next is mind blowing! The oil multiplied! She was able to sell the oil and make money.

In her obedience to the word of the prophet, she stepped into her mustard seed faith, and chose to trust, which in turn helped her unlock greater abundance. It catapulted her into greater faith to trust her Dad, her Heavenly Father, with what little she had in the natural realm. Through faith, she began to see with a Kingdom perspective. When her lenses began to shift, she stepped out in faith, trusting God to multiply the oil and flour, because guess what? In the third Heaven realm, there is no lack in the Kingdom. His ways are not our ways.

I have heard others say it, and I like to say it too: it's an upside-down Kingdom. We try to figure things out with our natural thinking, but in reality, surrendering to that mustard seed faith cracks open the heavens, and we begin to operate from the realm of the Spirit.

So, back to the lean season we were in. We had nothing...as in not even two pennies to rub together. I could feel the spirit of worry trying to creep in, but instead of allowing it to plague me as it had so much in the past, I chose to partner with Heaven and ask God a question. "What do I have in my hands that I can create wealth with?" Instantly, I heard Him say, "Bake pies." It was like a light bulb came on.

If you know me, you know I love to cook. I can't say I love baking, but I do like making most *any* food that brings a smile to people's faces, so this was going to involve vulnerability on my part by putting myself out there. But I did it; I put myself out there in the world of Facebook Marketplace and the various pages I'm on within our city, telling everyone I would be baking pies. The next thing I knew, order, after order, after order came in. My house felt like a pie factory, with flour everywhere and rolling out dough daily. My muscles were sore because I rolled out so much dough, but I was thankful and saw the hand of the Lord in it with me.

I ended up making about $300 from the sale of the pies, but it still wasn't enough to pay all the bills or buy Christmas presents for my four kids and my husband. I persevered in faith, and as I continued to step out, God did something miraculous.

It was November 24, a couple of days before Thanksgiving, and first thing in the morning, before I had even gotten out of bed, I got a text from an acquaintance:

"I bless your efforts—the Lord is going to multiply your income. I see you receiving more than you asked for. Well done starting with little...it'll turn into MUCH. Heaven's storehouses, open up over Mary and Peter, in Jesus' name!"

That morning, about 15 minutes after I read that text, I got another message from someone I didn't even know, but they had seen my advert for pies on Facebook. This person texted me and said, "God told me to give this to you." The "this" was a $500 financial gift. Later that same day, another friend had come by to pick up her four pies that her boss had ordered. She paid for them, giving a little extra, which we were very thankful for, and she left. After that, I left home to deliver the rest of the pies around the city to other customers, and the same woman called me, saying, "Mary you're going to want to meet me back at your house." I told her I would be there after I delivered the pies, which was going to take another hour or so. As I'm driving around, I'm wondering, "God what are you up to?"

I get home, walk in the door, and there she is, handing me a wad of cash. Her boss, who didn't even know us, felt led by the Lord to give us $1,000 cash! What?! The story doesn't end there. I was still taking a few pie orders, and now had some money for bills but not really enough to buy Christmas presents yet. My faith was high though, and I knew God was up to something.

A few days later, on the Saturday night following that Thanksgiving, we visited some friends who had come to our city to visit their kids who were in the ministry school here. It was late at night and I was torn between really wanting to see them but being tired and wishing to just go to bed. My heart was excited to spend time with our friends though for a couple of hours. After our time together, we got up to leave, and my friend handed me two checks—one from them and one from my friend's in-laws. I was like, "What are you doing, No!"

You see, sometimes you know you're still battling the poverty spirit when you have a hard time accepting and receiving things, especially money from people. To be honest, I still see this rise up in me from time to time. The poverty spirit can conceal itself at times as humility, but really, it's just pride masquerading as false humility wrapped up in a poverty mindset.

The poverty spirit can conceal itself at times as humility, but really it's just pride masquerading as false humility wrapped up in a poverty mindset.

It's okay to allow people to sow into you and not feel like a charity case. There are times and seasons for that. In this case, God was trying to break false humility and pride off of me! We hugged our friends and I sheepishly thanked them. As Peter was driving us home, I pulled out the checks, took one glance at them, and tears started streaming down my face. I was blown away. God had done it again. One check was for $1,000, and the other was for $250. *Wait a minute...God, what are You doing?* I was undone! In one week, God had given us over $3,000. Yes, God is that faithful when you choose to partner with Him, using the gifts and talents that you carry in your hands. Step out in faith and trust Him to meet you even half way.

When we choose to partner with Him with our gifts, He will come and meet us *all the way,* usually going above and beyond, exceedingly more than we could ask or even imagine. A lot of the time, He is just waiting for us to take the first step. With God, there is always enough. We may not get to go on that family vacation right away, but we can dream with God into it, and we can plan and save for it. Even if it's putting aside five, ten, or 20 dollars a week, which may seem little, but over time it grows into a vacation, into a nice Thanksgiving meal and Christmas presents for your kids, into a startup business, and more. The Kingdom of God is all about multiplication. You have to put seed in the ground to give God something to work with. My seed was stepping into mustard seed faith, partnering with God in that place of faith, choosing to trust Him while my circumstances said otherwise, and baking pies. It was choosing to look beyond the natural realm and ask Him, "What do I have in my hands?"

My heart's desire is for you to really understand this. It's not just for us, but it's for our kids to get this too. It's essential we teach them to pray for those things, and for their heart's desires, no matter how silly or insignificant it may seem (like my purple Walkman). Teaching them to step into mustard seed faith and trust God will cause a shift in the way they look at life. It will cause them to see beyond the natural realm and begin to look at things with eyes of the Spirit and with the eyes of faith. It will grow roots of truth in them, knowing He cares about it all and that He is for us. He is fun, and with Him all things are possible if we believe. It's believing in the things we can't see with our natural eyes because the realm of the Spirit is beyond the natural eyes.

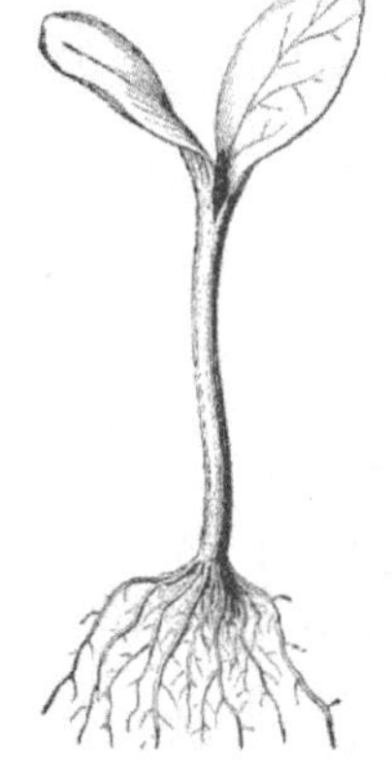

Chapter 4

Beyond The Natural Eyes

In the Cambridge Essential English Dictionary, the definition for faith (paraphrased) is:

Believing that someone or something deserves to be trusted.

In Hebrews 11:1 it says,

Now faith is the certainty of things hoped for, a proof of things not seen.

God is always moving, and He will even move Heaven and earth on our behalf to bring forth life's possibilities. Whether we can see it or not, we just have to purposefully decide two things in our hearts: that He cares for us as His son or daughter and that He is good. And by faith we believe it. We set our eyes on Him so we can hope and see beyond the natural realm. God is faithful and trustworthy! It takes faith to trust.

The dictionary's definition for trust is,

"Belief that someone or something is reliable, good, honest, effective, etc."

Many of you, like me, may have grown up without a father. For me, this gave a distorted view of what a good father really looks like. Also having a horrible stepfather for some of my younger years made it even more challenging. My circumstances made it harder to believe or trust in how loving and good God really is as a Father. On the outside, I seemed fine and acted like I had the perfect family, yet on the inside, I was a mess.

On the outside, most of us mask our emotions, but beyond the natural eye, the Spirit of God sees right through the mask. I was really good at masking my emotions. Hiding behind smiles, I had a people-pleasing personality. The truth was, I was very shy and afraid of people. In school or at Sunday school I didn't speak unless spoken to, which was something drilled into us as children. I rarely spoke the truth about my true feelings or desires, and those all got placed behind a passive-aggressive personality. People were not to be trusted, especially adults, and I didn't think anyone had my best interests in mind or even cared. As a child, yes, I would smile, laugh, and be the peacemaker so to speak, yet inwardly, I constantly withdrew and hid away my heart. I may have felt like I was hiding, but the reality is we can never truly hide, especially from God. In Psalm 139:7–8, David says,

Where can I go from your Spirit? Where can I flee from your presence? If I go up to the Heavens, you are there; if I make my bed in the depths, you are there.

He sees us—every part. He sees the anger, He sees the shame, He sees the hurt, the unforgiveness, and the dirt. He sees our desire to be close, but not fully knowing how to get there. He sees the floundering, the procrastination. He sees when we self-medicate, step into being a workaholic or an alcoholic, and when we zone out on a gaming system, that drug, a pill, porn, masturbation, romance novels, cleaning frenzies, trying to control everything, made-up house work, binging on food, binge watching that Netflix TV show, scrolling on our phones for hours and hours instead of leaning into our pain and turning to Him. He sees the truth behind everything we do. Everything done *in secret*...He sees it all!

> He sees the truth behind everything we do. Everything done in secret He sees it all.

We need to allow the Spirit of God to journey with us into the secret places of our hearts—the ones we so secretly try to hide from the rest of the world. We need to let Him journey with us into the many roads of our heart to bring truth to our reality. The Bible says in John 8:32 it's His truth—God's truth—that sets us free.

And you will know the truth, and the truth will make you free.

If you don't purposely connect to the One with the ability to set you free, you won't ever *truly* be free. You will always feel like something, a piece of you, is missing. I know I did. People are body, spirit, and soul, and our body (including our mind) and soul need to be led by our spirit. The realm of the spirit is not usually available to the natural eye; it's *beyond* the natural eye. The spirit realm is seen and understood as you lean into Him and grow in relationship with Him, getting to know and trust Him as a good Father, faithful Friend, beautiful King, and sweet Lover.

The closer you become to Him, the better you will understand and know His heart for you. As He gently whispers them, you will know the truths of what He speaks over you. It's in this place where the ears of your heart are open to hear Him rightly and truly receive

Him. Did you know your heart has ears? Well, I imagine in the Spirit it does.

When Solomon prayed for wisdom, surprisingly, he did not use the word "wisdom." What he prayed for, according to the ESV translation, in 1 Kings 3:9 was,

...an understanding mind to govern your people, that I may discern between good and evil.

In his affirmation of Solomon's prayer, God summarized it as a request for...

...understanding to discern what is right. —1 Kings 3:11

Something interesting about this is found within the original language used in 1 Kings 3. The ESV translation of *understanding mind* in verse 9 and *understanding* in verse 10 translates into a Hebrew verb (shama) which really means *to hear.* Considering this, the two lines (verses 9 and 11) translated more literally say,

Give to your servant a ***hearing heart****, to judge your people, to discern between good and evil ... you have asked for yourself to discern, to hear judgment.*

In order to hear with your heart, you have to purposely take your mustard seed of faith, choose to trust Him, lean in, and seek God and His voice. You have to consciously block out all other voices in order to tune-in to your Heavenly Father and make that heart connection. Block all voices, including the voice of fear.

Fear often masquerades as wisdom, and can cause you to make a decision that feels safe or comfortable. These kinds of decisions may seem good, logical even, but those decisions might not necessarily be the wisdom of God speaking. When you lean into Him and allow that heart connection to happen with Him, you won't fear. Knowing you're hearing God's wisdom instead, which is louder than the voice of fear, settles you. Then, you can step into trust, which will walk you into blind, bold faith.

Why do I say *blind* faith? Because it's seeing beyond what you can see with your natural eye. We don't see everything, but He does. Will we trust Him and listen?

Pursue His presence and don't stop till you find Him. You might be asking yourself, *How do I do that? How do I really pursue His presence?* I have found through the years, that He is a person whose presence is tangible. To cultivate His presence, first find Him by stepping into that little mustard seed faith, which leads to trust. When you choose to begin to trust, He can lead you into greater faith and understanding of who He really is. As you walk into trust, your faith ignites in greater measure, and your desire for more of Him grows.

When I grew in greater understanding of this, I couldn't wait to be with Him. I began to realize my desire for Him wasn't bound to just Sunday at church, and neither is yours. It's not bound by Wednesday night youth groups, midweek services, or even by your 30 minutes of devotional time in the morning. There are no boundaries or constraints in how you do relationship with Jesus. My own desire for Him grew, and His presence around me became tangible. I began to find myself praying at different times of the day and dialoging with Him while washing dishes, cooking, or driving, and many times that 30-minute devotional time turned into longer periods of just sitting with Him, talking and listening. Yes, talk to Him like He is sitting in the chair across from you. After all, He is a person. It may feel weird at first, but trust me, it becomes amazing!

Talking to God through prayer develops intimacy. Out of intimacy flows increase. As more breakthrough happens, acceleration happens, and greater revelation and fruitfulness begins to take place. Find Him in the Bible, which is the written Word of God and the very breath of God. He will speak to you as you read. Your heart will be in tune with what He is saying, and answers will jump off the pages as He kisses you with His Word. Take walks with Him, or sit in the quiet with Him.

I say *in the quiet* because the world is a noisy place. From the time we get up to the time we go to bed, we have our phones, our radios, our TVs all playing something. We have the noise of bustling streets, restaurants, busyness of work, and life, and people. As much as I love my children, and if you are anything like me, you always have the clamoring of your kids. A hundred times a day, you hear, "Hey Mom, Mom, MOMMYYYYY!" There are days when I have to just get away and seek out the quiet to reconnect with God and myself.

So, I want to challenge you to get quiet. One thing I love to do is to walk with no earbuds or headphones so I can listen to the sound of the nature around me. I watch the birds fly to a nearby tree and perch in the branches. I watch the squirrels chase each other, or fish jumping in the river, or ducks dunking in the water for their morning breakfast as I stroll along the trail by the Sacramento River near my house.

If I'm not walking, I also love to sit in my backyard and sip on a nice cup of hot coffee or tea. I love to sit in nature in the woods, or be out on a boat on the lake. Sometimes I go fishing, and I talk to Him while mindlessly standing there in the water, fishing – yes, I love fishing. I talk to Him on walking trails, or on the beach.

Sometimes I will just sit in my bedroom in complete silence and allow my heart and mind to rest while I meditate on Him. Sometimes I'll quietly play instrumental worship music and read the Word. Sometimes I pull out my guitar and play for an audience of one, only to Him. I hope you're getting the point; just get quiet with your inward thoughts, and seek out alone time with Him.

As much as I love to be alone with Him, I have also found that sometimes finding more of Him doesn't require you to be alone. You can also find Him by seeking out leaders and peers who have cultivated the type of relationship with God that you also want. Your relationship doesn't have to look like theirs. However, if you know they have more of Him in ways that you desire, go after that and seek these people out! When you seek them out and allow people like this to speak into your life, they can help train and lead you to His heart and into more of His presence. And sometimes things can be more caught than taught. When I am around people often, I learn and pick things up without realizing it right away. While we should all seek to be our authentic selves, it's still important to seek out key leaders and glean all you can from them.

From the time I was 12 and into my teens and beyond, I had the privilege of having an awesome woman of God named Beth in my life. She was totally sent from God, and she became like a sister, friend, and spiritual mother to me. To this day, we are still in each other's lives. We are more like family than friends, so much so, my kids call her Auntie Beth.

I absolutely loved being around her vibrant Italian personality, and I was always watching her life, learning so much by just being around her. When I would spend the night at her house, I would watch as she loved on her husband Bill and her children. Every morning when I got up and walked out of the bedroom, I would see her sitting there, with her Bible cracked open, spending time with Jesus, journaling and praying.

It seemed she always woke up early to meet with Jesus. She prioritized time with Him, and seeing that on a daily basis grew a hunger in me to be with Him and pursue His heart too. It shaped my understanding of who God is and the simplicity and beauty of what's available when we make room for Him in our lives. I watched her as she would stand in faith and contend for things. I watched her trust God in the midst of hard situations with their business, with family, or other different relationships. I watched as she stepped out in blind faith, trusted God, and contended for her awesome house, and they ended up getting an incredible Jesus deal.

Letting her into my inner world and being brought into hers gave me an up-close and personal, front-row-seat kind of view, seeing how she lived her daily life and loved Jesus in it. This, in turn, caused a hunger in me to be more like her...or so I thought at the time. When I got older, I realized the deep desire wasn't really to be like her; it was to be more like Jesus who I saw in her and shined through her.

I wanted more of Jesus. I wanted to know Him how she intimately knew and loved Him. His love coming through her drew me to Him. She knew how to love well and trust God in the hard things. She used to always say what her dad Hank taught her to say: "Can't is not in your vocabulary!" and that statement is so true. After all, the Bible does tell us in Philippians 4:13,

I CAN do ALL things through Christ who strengthens me.
(Emphasis mine.)

Beth believed beyond the natural eye, she trusted in God, and she chose to live from the realm of the spirit. Her trust and belief that God would always come through and her strength in the Lord helped grow me into the person I am today. Beth also was known for saying, "Speak life." She has Italian blood, so she was always very animated when she would say it! It was drilled into me so much, that even to this day I say those things to my kids from time to time. "Can't is not in your vocabulary," and her other famous words, "Speak life!"

Proverbs 18:21 puts it this way:

The tongue has the power of life and death.

Your words can either speak *life*, or your words can speak *death*. Through the years, I have heard it said that our tongues are like a rudder of a ship (James 3:4–5). What we speak out can steer the course of our destiny. For instance, if you constantly say things like, "I hate ________" (fill in the blank), or, "I'm so stupid, I'm never going to get ahead, I'm never going to lose weight, I'm never going to have enough money," etc., guess what? You are prophesying over your future and creating that world around you! If you say or hear those thoughts in your mind and fill your life constantly with them, then you have a major battle going on. If those words are a part of your daily life, stop and think about your life. Could your life possibly be the way it is because of what you've spoken out? Our words are so incredibly powerful.

Your words can either speak life, or your words can speak death.

Sometimes words like this are normal to us. It's just how we grew up, consistently thinking and hearing all those negative things come out of the mouths of the adults around us. Usually, if we heard those kinds of words from the mouths of our own parents, it became a part of our core identity. However, wrong thinking can be reversed—and needs to be. We have to retrain and renew our minds with the Word of God—with truth to think like Christ—over our past and present situations, and over ourselves. Romans 12:2 tells us to,

...be transformed by the renewing of your mind.

If you throw out the negative self-talk, who are you really? Stop and ask this: "God, who do You say I am?" Who *He* says you are is the real truth. Your natural-realm perspective may feel like it's truth, but remember I said our feelings sometime lie to us? When you look beyond the natural eye and beyond this natural realm and partner with the realm of the spirit, the Spirit of God, He has the ultimate truth. He knows *you* better than you know yourself!

When I was younger, I had an oppressive, negative, and worrisome bent in my personality and speech. I grew up with my mother and other family members often speaking negative things around me, over me, and to me. Beth used to say it was like I walked around with a dark cloud over my head. I hadn't really learned the power of my words until I got around her. I didn't realize my words could create negative or positive worlds around me. Being around her taught me so much. I not only learned about the truth of who Jesus was, I also began to learn how to love myself.

Even though she and her family weren't perfect, they were as close to perfect as anyone I knew. Being with them taught me a lot about health and beauty from the inside out—and the outside in. I learned how to do family well and that family didn't have to be sad, depressing, or scary.

When we take that mustard seed of faith, step into trust, and allow safe people into our lives who will speak life into us, over us, and will reveal the heart of the Heavenly Father to us, our heart will grow in faith and begin to change. As faith grows, its roots begin to take hold, and they grow bigger into the foundations of God's truth supporting your life. None of this is magical; we have to lean in and do the work, but it will happen. Over time you'll realize your foundation is no longer shaky as your root system starts growing deeper and deeper into a solid, healthy foundation.

Don't be afraid to pursue spiritual mothers and fathers. Although they will *never* be perfect, sometimes God will use people like spiritual mothers and fathers to teach you about perfect love found only in Him. I learned I don't have to fear God, and that He alone is perfect. I learned this from people like Beth and her husband Bill, and others He sent across my path, through various stages of my life through the years. I also learned how to trust and love others well because of her persistence and pursuit of my heart. She never gave up on me, and to this day, I choose to model that for those God gives me to pour into.

Trusting people when you've been hurt takes faith. In my younger years, I had a hard time trusting people because of the abuse in my life. I really didn't want people to get close to me, so I would either try to make myself small and unnoticed, put-up walls, or purposefully, or sometimes unknowingly, push people away. For me, it came down to learning to let love into every crevasse of my heart.

Remember, God is love. The Father's love always leads to repentance, and it will lead you to forgiveness as well. If you forgive the people who've hurt you, He'll take away the pain they caused you. Choose to trust Him and His goodness in the process, even if your feelings don't match up to what you're doing or speaking out by faith yet. He is always moving beyond the natural eye. If you set your faith in motion, eventually your feelings will follow. Now, let's take a moment to pray and ask God for a fresh start in the journey of trust.

Pray With Me

Jesus,
I ask You right now to reach in and touch the broken places of my heart, places where I've had a hard time trusting people and trusting You. Please forgive me.
Help me to learn how to allow Your love into the crevasses of my heart so that I can love You and love other people well.

Now, speak to your heart...and remember, your heart has ears.

Heart,
I give you permission to let fear, and the fear of trusting myself, and trusting others go, in Jesus' name.
I give you permission to feel again and to trust again.
I give you permission to feel love and to be loved.

Jesus,
Please show me the people in my world who are safe, who I can trust, and who You want me to be in relationship with.
I know that with You, I am never alone, and that You desire to bring people into my life who will help bring me closer to You because You created me for connection.
Forgive me for pushing people away and for shutting people out of my life.
Thank you that every day is a new day with You.
It's a new day to breathe You in and breath You out.
I choose to trust You, Jesus!
Amen!

Now, begin to daily thank Jesus for the right relationships to come into your life—relationships that will build you up in Him and not tear you down. Make daily, godly declarations around this. What are godly declarations? They are words we release and speak out that are biblical truths. They align with Heaven and create an atmosphere for change. I don't know who coined this phrase, but like I said earlier, our words can create worlds.

So, what world, what atmosphere, do you want to live in?

Proverbs 18:21 says,

The tongue has the power of life and death.

What you and I believe matters, and this verse means that the stakes are high. Our words really do release things into the atmosphere. We either speak death, or we speak life over ourselves and our situations. Our words can build ourselves and others up or tear them down. They can build our businesses up or tear them down. They can build our families strong or make them weak. I think you're getting the picture.

Begin to speak life over yourself!

Speak life over your situation.
Speak life over your body if you have sickness.
Speak life over your financial situation.
Speak life over your business(s).
Speak life over your dreams.
Speak life over the salvation of your loved one(s).
Speak life over your lost relationships—ones your heart is broken and grieving over.
Speak life over your marriage.

Speak life over your heart that endured abuse and trauma.
Speak life over your prodigal son or daughter.

The negativity or "the cloud" that followed me in my younger years was a thought pattern. It had to be reversed in my life, and its origins were due to my upbringing and the trauma I endured. Even though I had been raised in the church, I really had no idea how to speak life over myself. Gradually, I learned how to do this. My words began to shift my beliefs, and they started creating new worlds around me. I began to feel lighter, I began to feel joy, and I began to *hope*. Sometimes when we've lived a certain way for a long time, those thought patterns take time to reverse, and the only way to reverse it is by creating new ones.

You know what's wild and so amazing? It's scientifically proven that if you do things for 65 days or longer, new patterns in your brain begin to form. Everyone is different though, and it could take you 65 days or maybe a little longer. It really depends on how much we lean in and go after change.

While I know God can do quick works in people's hearts, it never happens randomly on its own or in some whimsical way. It really takes stepping out in our mustard seed of faith, partnering with truth, and trusting in a good, good God. God can begin to train you on how to break those bad habits, bad speech (even cussing), and negative ways of thinking. Habits are the brain's internal pathways. A lot of our daily actions are automatic because we've trained ourselves to go on autopilot. Your brain likes autopilot; that's how it conserves energy. For better or worse, our habits shape us.

God can begin to train you on how to break those bad habits, bad speech, and negative ways of thinking.

Breaking a bad habit ultimately is about rewiring your brain. Habits are found in an area of your brain called the basal ganglia. The more often you perform an action or behave a certain way, the more it gets physically wired into your brain. This amazing adaptive quality of your brain is known as neuroplasticity. Your brain forms neuronal connections based on what you do repeatedly in your life, both good and bad. Every time you act in the same way, a specific neuronal pattern is stimulated and becomes strengthened in your brain.

If you want to change negative neural pathways in your brain (formed by bad habits) into positive ones, then you should have a clear exit strategy to break out of the bad brain patterns that bind you to the negativity. You might be wondering, *Where or how can I even start?* Start with your words. Your words are your exit sign—your way into greater mental and heart health. They *are* powerful! Declare truth, and let thanksgiving always be on your lips. If you don't know how to start this, below I have put together a few declarations of truth you can speak over yourself.

Let's start here:

- I am loved and I am capable of love.
- I declare I am a carrier of Your presence, and God, You love to spend time with me.
- I declare that I never lose favor with You, God, and that I am always loved as Your daughter/son.
- I thank you, God, that I am fearfully and wonderfully made, and that You are for me and not against me.
- I thank you, Father, that I am Your precious daughter/son, and that I have access to everything Your Kingdom has to offer because You are my good, good Father.

- I thank you, God, that right now, You are moving mountains on my behalf.
- I speak to the mountain of _______ (fill in the blank), and I tell it to be removed in Jesus' name!
- You, O Lord, You are my Provider, and You provide *all* of my financial needs. In You there is no lack.
- I thank you, God, that I am the head and not the tail.
- I thank you, God, that I am an overcomer of shame.
- I thank you, God, that You are always with me, therefore I am never really alone.
- I declare and thank You, God, that my family and I walk in the fruit of Your Spirit, and we are full of love, joy, peace, patience, kindness, gentleness, self-control, Your goodness, and Your favor.
- I thank you, God, that I am a person full of faith and am not afraid to trust You!

When you wake up in the morning, start your day with thankfulness. In the quiet of your heart, as you are still laying warm and cozy in your bed, while you are staring at the back of your eyelids, say, "Good morning, Holy Spirit, I love You. Today is going to be a great day!" It will set the pace of your day.

My son Luke used to complain almost every day about going to school, citing how school was hard, he didn't like it, etc. So, I began to go after that. Every morning when I would take him to school and walk him across the playground to his classroom, I would have him do one declaration to help change his belief that school was hard. I also wanted it to set the pace and heart posture for his day, so I would have him repeat this after me:

“Today is a great day. Good things are going to happen to me today.
Today is a day of victory and breakthrough,
and I am filled with the wisdom and knowledge of God.
Therefore, I am smart, I am loved, and I love school!”

Things began to shift the more he repeated this—day in and day out, week after week—and after a while, instead of him telling me how much he didn’t like school and feeling anxious and stressed out about it, he started to change. His heart posture was no longer negative; it became more positive and happier. His heart was finally at peace. Having him repeat this every day shifted his mindset and changed his beliefs over time, and I still have him say this daily. Some days, if I accidently forget to do it and we’re almost to His school, Luke will say, “Wait, Mom, our declaration.” I love how he always says how much he loves school now. I love how he gets in the car after school and usually says, “Mom, I had a great day today!”

Your words *are* powerful! Declarations are not magical, but they are powerful. They can move mountains in any situation as you attach your faith to them, even if it’s a mustard seed-sized faith. God will meet you in the journey. By now, you’re getting the picture and the point here. Let your words create life into your day-to-day world.

Beyond the natural eye, your words carry your mustard seed of faith into great trust, and from this place, it sprouts, you grow your roots, and it can change your reality. As your roots grow, you build a stronger foundation, and in turn, your mustard seed of faith grows a tree that will shape your future. Your tree will stretch its branches far and wide to house a legacy, just as it has for me, just as it has for many of the men, women, and patriarchs in the Bible, and just as it can for you!

Chapter 5

In The Midst Of The Reeds

I really love the history of the Bible and learning about the patriarchs and matriarchs of old and the legacy they left behind. When I say patriarchs and legacy, all I have to do is mention *Hebrews*, and just saying it is like scaling the tallest mustard tree of legacy. The book of Hebrews in the Bible has some of the greatest *who's who* famous men and women of faith, mainly found in chapter 11—known as *the faith chapter*. In my lifetime, I can't even count how many times I've read it or heard somebody preach on it.

Hebrews chapter 11 is so rich and full. On a good day, I've read it and felt so encouraged by it, then somehow felt ready to conquer the world. Yet on a bad day, I've read it and somehow have felt discouraged and inadequate. *How in the world could I ever measure up and have faith like these people?* Some of you may be laughing, as this totally resonates with you. I seriously would find myself sometimes just begging God to just give me an ounce of faith like those great men and women of old. I didn't understand that I already had mustard seed faith inside of me, and all I had to do was step into it.

As I've walked through life and grown older, I've seen God answer many prayers as I learned to step into that small seed of faith. He's surprised me and come through for me countless times, and you know what? I am an ordinary person—just like the heroes and heroines of Hebrews 11. Yes! Believe it or not, they were ordinary people on this earth like you and me. If He has done it for them and for me, He'll do it for you too!

They may not seem ordinary to us today, yet they were. The older I get, I realize more and more just how each and every one of those people in Hebrews were totally ordinary. I'm sure they had their own struggles with questioning their mustard seed faith and with trusting God too; however, more often than not, they saw the hand of God deliver them. They saw the hand of God provide for them, fight for them, and comfort them in amazing ways. He came through for them in ways that defy the natural realm to bring them into a place of simply trusting Him. They saw His goodness and couldn't deny the reality of who He is. He is a good, good Father!

When we think of people of faith in the Bible, we often think about men like Noah who built the ark in obedience to God. During his building process, people were laughing at him, mocking him, and scoffing constantly, making fun of him for being "obedient" to God. Well, at least that's how it was until it rained (Genesis 6:9–9:28)! Then, there was young David, who was probably laughed at when he came out to fight Goliath in Saul's armor (which was way too big for Him). He told Saul, "I can't fight with all this!" so he took it off and stepped out in his mustard seed faith. Taking his slingshot, he fought the Philistine's giant, Goliath, with no armor and only five stones, and he won the victory for the Israelites (1 Samuel 17:38–53).

They saw His goodness and couldn't deny the reality of who He is.

Let's not forget Gideon who conquered the Midianite's huge army with just 300 men. Talk about a crazy, inspiring story (Judges 7:4-16)!

There are so many amazing, heroic men in the Bible, all well worth the read. However, I want to also point out and draw special attention to the *women* of faith. Women, this chapter is for you. If you're a man reading this book, keep reading. I know you'll get something out of it too.

When we Google "Women of faith in the Bible" or "Heroines in the Bible" or "Amazing women of the Bible," the highlighted ones, such as Mary the mother of Jesus whose life held great honor, with a great calling that also required great suffering. She was a virgin when she first conceived, and because of the Jewish culture she was raised in, I'm sure she had to endure ridicule and scorn because of her pregnancy out of wedlock. She held onto her trust in God and the promise given to her when she had a supernatural encounter with the angel Gabriel. Mary walked in faith to believe for the impossible. She was a willing servant and a young woman of great purity and honor in the eyes of God (*most scholars believe she was around 15 years old*), who trusted her completely. She was walking by mustard seed faith, which released greater faith to trust in the word of the Lord, and in turn, it helped her to stand on His promise. Having that faith to stand led her to walk into her greatest calling—carrying the Savior of the world (Luke 1:26–56). I'm sure her greatest joy was being the mother of Jesus, the One who would die to save mankind.

Another Old Testament woman was Ruth, who had lost her husband and was living with her widowed mother-in-law Naomi. Unfortunately, Ruth had lost her husband without a chance to bear children, at least that is what some scholars believe. Some have proposed that she may have been barren, but whatever the circumstances were, I'm sure we can agree that the emotional pain Ruth must have been in was intense. Childbearing in Ruth's culture was of upmost importance. It was like a badge of honor to have children.

In many cultures still today, this is true. In East Africa, where I spent 16 years as a missionary, I noticed this to be very true amongst the different tribal village women. In my opinion, Ruth had such an incredible and remarkable faith for such a young believer. She didn't allow negative words to penetrate her heart. She showed a faith that caused her to believe there was still a purpose for her life. She trusted God and walked honorably with others and had *great* faith to believe that God was who He says He is.

She also had faith to believe that God would provide for her and her mother-in-law Naomi. Ruth walked with honor and a servant's heart as she served Naomi. Her faith to trust God led her to become the wife of Boaz—a wealthy, prestigious man who owned land who was able to care for her and her mother-in-law. Because of her faithfulness (not because of her works), I believe God saw to it that Ruth would step into His blessings. Going through the door of trust led her into greater faith. Her faith led her to a position of honor as the wife of a wealthy business man and eventually, a mother who bore a son named Obed. Obed grew up and became the father of Jesse, and Jesse became the father of King David. It was through her lineage that the King of Kings would come—King Jesus Christ of Nazareth, the Savior of the world (Ruth 2–4).

Here is another very famous name drop: Esther. Many people know the story of Esther, but if not, you can read it in the Bible in the book of Esther (chapters 1–10, which is found in the Old Testament). She was a Jewish orphan girl raised by her uncle Mordecai, and later, she became the queen. Esther was a remarkable woman who was willing to risk her life to save the Jewish Nation—her own people. She was a woman of principle, willing to put the lives of others ahead of even her own life. She's an outstanding example of serving others even under the most stressful circumstances. With her mustard seed faith, she stepped into trusting God and moved mountains. In the natural realm, she put herself in harm's way, but by faith, she trusted to believe that the hand of God would supernaturally protect her *for such a time as this*. Her simple seed of faith grew over time into a huge, deeply rooted tree of trust and faith in God. And through that, she saw the hand of God move on her behalf as she stepped out, risking her own life to save a nation.

I could go on and on about these women, but I want to highlight and give time and attention to one other incredible woman of faith who, in my opinion, often gets overlooked. All of the Sunday school stories I heard never taught about this remarkable woman. She has piqued my curiosity many times when reading Hebrews 11. This mysterious heroine's name is only used in some Bible translations, but God deemed her important enough to honor her in the *who's who* book of Hebrews.

Nothing is expounded on about her directly in the three books of the Bible she's mentioned in. Because one of my goals for writing this book is to highlight stories of trust that unlocks greater faith, her name jumped off the pages of Hebrews chapter 11. You're probably thinking, *Alright already, Mary...what is her name?!* Drum roll please...

Her name is Jochebed!

In your mind's eye, go with me to Egypt. Jochebed enters the scene. Can you see it? Dirt roads that are a reddish, rust-looking color are filled with the hustle and bustle of everyday people in ancient

Egypt. People work their fields, make mud bricks to build houses, women tend to their families and take care of their babies and households. Can you see them? They're cooking over smokey fires, most likely set up outside of their tents or mud-bricked houses. As you walk down the road, your nose catches whiffs of food cooking. Some of the wealthier women who owned businesses sit on the side of the road, weaving baskets or maybe even selling food, such as breads, choice fruits, and vegetables. The poorer women are bent over, working in harsh, back-breaking labor, helping their husbands harvest in the fields. You can smell fish; the waters of the Nile River run through this area with its marshy tall grass. Women and children carry baskets on their heads and come to the water's edge to bathe or wash and scrub clothes by hand.

Can you see it?

Okay. good. Now...welcome to Egypt. Welcome to a glimpse of what Jochebed's life probably looked like in this ancient land.

Come with me into the book of Exodus.

The Birth of Moses: Exodus 2:1–10

Now a man from the house of Levi went and married a daughter of Levi. The woman conceived and bore a son; and when she saw that he was beautiful, she hid him for three months. But when she could hide him no longer, she got him a wicker basket and covered it over with tar and pitch. Then she put the child into it and set it among the reeds by the bank of the Nile.

His sister stood at a distance to find out what would happen to him.

The daughter of Pharaoh came down to bathe at the Nile, with her maidens walking alongside the Nile; and she saw the basket among the reeds and sent her maid, and she brought it to her. When she opened it, she saw the child, and behold, the boy was crying. And she had pity on him and said, "This is one of the Hebrews' children."

Then his sister said to Pharaoh's daughter, "Shall I go and call a nurse for you from the Hebrew women that she may nurse the child for you?"

Pharaoh's daughter said to her, "Go ahead."

So, the girl went and called the child's mother. Then Pharaoh's daughter said to her, "Take this child away and nurse him for me and I will give you your wages."

So, the woman took the child and nursed him. The child grew, and she brought him to Pharaoh's daughter and he became her son. And she named him Moses, and said, "Because I drew him out of the water."

I absolutely love this story. Albeit heartbreaking, you can still see God's hand in the midst of it all. So, how do we know Moses's mother's name was Jochebed? Let's take a look at two more verses.

Amram married his father's sister Jochebed, and she bore him Aaron and Moses; and the length of Amram's life was one hundred and thirty-seven years. —Exodus 6:20

The name of Amram's wife was Jochebed, the daughter of Levi, who was born to Levi in Egypt; and she bore to Amram: Aaron and Moses and their sister Miriam. —Numbers 26:59

So, we know that Moses's biological father's name was Amram, and he married Jochebed, and she was a mother of three. Moses already had two older siblings when he was born. Women in Bible days were very busy women. No, I don't mean just because they were having sex and having lots of children. The truth is, in their day-to-day lives, they were busy; life was full and life was hard. They didn't have the ease of the many amenities we have in today's modern world. They worked hard from the time they got up in the morning until they finally went to bed at night.

As I took you to ancient Egypt in your mind's eye, I could visualize the women from Tanzania where I lived. I imagine that many of the ancient Egyptian women were like the East African village women. You work from the time you wake up to the time you go to bed. You get up and start your fire over twigs, milk your goats or cow for some fresh milk for the day (because you don't have a refrigerator), fetch a pail of water to boil for some hot tea, and then cook the porridge for your children's breakfast. After that, you sometimes walk miles with your children to fetch more water for bathing, washing clothes, for cooking the evening meal, etc., only to walk back in the dry heat, carrying gallons of water on your head and/or possibly big logs for more firewood. Next, after you milk the cows and goats again, you then let them out to find a bit of green grass and food. After that, you might find yourself cultivating your garden, harvesting what you can, doing your sewing projects, making trinkets to sell at the market or even to travelers passing through, cutting firewood to sell, and then scraping together food for the evening meal. Whew, I'm sure you feel tired just reading all of that...I know I am! All in a day's work. We truly are spoiled in the Western world.

Okay, now back to Jochebed. What a woman! I think I built enough of a case to point out that she most likely lived in a much tougher life situation compared to our world today. She had to have faith just to raise her children, let alone survive in her crazy world. I believe her courage and her incredible trust in God resulted in her strong faith, and this is why God deemed her worthy to be placed among the heroines of faith in Hebrews 11:23.

So, here is this woman who has two young children. Her eldest daughter Miriam, was about ten years of age, and then there was Aaron who was possibly around age three. Now, here she is, pregnant. What should have been a joyous occasion turned sour really fast. At Pharaoh's command, all Hebrew baby boys were to be terminated upon birth. *What the heck*? Can you even imagine her suspense? Jochebed had no idea if she was having a boy or a girl. *What will I do if it's a boy? Will he be torn from my arms and thrown into the Nile River? God, HELP me! God, my heart, I can't even go there!*

Fast forward to the day she gives birth to Moses. Oh, the joy, the fear, and yet the sorrow that must have gripped her heart. As a mother of five children myself (*our baby boy Asher is in Heaven*), I can't imagine birthing a child, getting to kiss their little face, looking into their sweet eyes, nuzzle my nose into their neck, smell that newborn baby smell, feel their soft baby skin and their tiny hand inside mine, and then suddenly lose them or be forced to give them up, or even worse...they get snatched out of my arms.

I am a *bona fide* Mama Bear when it comes to my four living children. *No one had better harm them!* If need be, I would fight for their lives. Many of you women can relate to what I'm saying. There is a special bond that happens with each baby as you carry them within you. Each one is being formed uniquely, and each one is being fearfully and wonderfully made during those long and sometimes hard nine months. Then, they are born into this world and delivered into your arms. *Cue the tears, yes, I'm crying!* It's so special and hard to truly put into words, the feelings that wash over you every time you give birth.

Jochebed had given birth before, so I'm sure she felt all the new mom feels, but yet, the gut-wrenching, heart-tearing truth of

Pharaoh's decree was still there, staring her in the face. In those first moments as she held Moses and put him to her chest, with him suckling at her breast, I imagine she just simply listened to him breathe and nurse. I'm sure she studied his tiny lips, pulled him close, and smelled him, savoring his baby smell. Just like every mother who is mesmerized with their new born, maybe she sang to him while cradling him tightly. You all know what I'm talking about; those newborn smells are priceless.

In that moment, she saw him in all his beauty! The Bible says three times that she saw her baby boy Moses and was overcome with his beauty. In Exodus 2:2, Acts 7:20, and Hebrews 11:23, we read that he was a *fine child*, he was *beautiful in God's sight*, and *they saw that the child was beautiful*. So, it's obvious they thought he was beautiful and could clearly see he was marked by God. Moses was no ordinary child. As her baby boy laid in her lap, I believe Jochebed felt with her motherly intuition that he was destined for greatness and had been specially sent by God. Knowing and purposing that in her heart, this led her to take her mustard seed faith and step into trust, believing God would preserve his life. But how? If Moses was anything like my babies, he would cry and wouldn't keep quiet, especially when he was hungry. How would she keep him hidden? How could she possibly preserve His life?

Ladies, let's face it. With a newborn in this situation, we would have been worried sick! I'm sure Jochebed had those days too at times, yet somehow she stepped into this place of fierceness, of total trust. In the trusting, her worrying was diminished. God gave her great faith and a plan. I'm pretty sure she didn't hear a *thus saith the Lord* kind of plan. Maybe she did, maybe she didn't, but however He spoke to her, it steadied her heart to be fully obedient as she stepped out. I believe that as she anchored herself in the Lord, she would get ideas of what to do and trusted that God was leading her. A wise older woman once told me,

"Mary, trust God inside of you! The steps of the righteous are ordered of the Lord, and if you are in Him, you just have to step, putting one foot in front of the other. Hold onto Him and step out and keep walking! He will lead!"

Jochebed's trust led her into greater faith to let her God—*your God*, the God of Israel, the God of the miraculous stories she grew up hearing about—lead her.

When the Mama Bear rises up and chooses to trust, there is no fear! Jochebed leaned in, she listened, and she followed. She defied all cultural rightness and threw it out the window. Some people would have thought her crazy. Just like Jesus' mother Mary, I'm sure they ridiculed Jochebed too, or maybe she did it all in secret so no one knew? However she did it, she did it! Like Mary, I'm sure she held these things in her heart and dared to trust the voice of the One inside of her.

When the Mama Bear rises up and chooses to trust, there is no fear!

We know she stepped into a place of trust with her act of faith: making a baby basin, or basket if you will. She worked hard, making it from plaited reeds, which some believe were protection against the crocodiles. Now, I can hear you thinking, *Wait...back up. What? CROCS?* Yes, I'm serious! I've been to Egypt and sailed on the Nile River. While I was there, I never saw a crocodile, but I knew they existed because our guide made sure we knew they were there.

Rumor has it, the crocs in the Nile River can get up to 16.5 feet long. That is half the size of a school bus, and they can weigh in at

1,500 lbs. Isn't that just wild? Wow! This woman Jochebed would have been charged for child abuse or murder in today's world for putting her baby boy in the Nile River in a basket. Who in their right mind puts a baby into a river with crocodiles? I'll tell you who...a woman who has had an encounter with the Living God, one who knows the voice of her God, one who trusts and steps out in faith *knowing* her God will come through. That's who!

Here is Jochebed with her basin, after coating it with tar and pitch to make it waterproof, she takes her baby boy, looks into his beautiful face, and (I imagine with tears streaming down her face) she whispers, "I love you," over and over again as she gazes into his eyes and sees the promises of God. I'm sure she sees his destiny, and in her heart, albeit broken, she trusts in the Lord because He is so, so good. She knows her God is the same yesterday, today, and forever.

As she leans over, kisses her baby boy's face, kisses his lips, holds him tight, smells him one last time (or so she thought), and then lays him in the basket, most likely as a mother so in love with her baby, hot tears rolled down her cheeks. They were probably rushing down her face so fast at this point that she could hardly see. I can only imagine that Jochebed's tears were the kind of tears where you're literally snot crying everywhere. Yet in that moment, I'm sure the peace of God began to flood her soul and heart. As she released him into the midst of the reeds on the banks of the Nile River, I imagine she, too, purposed this in her heart just as Mary did:

Be it unto me according to your will, O Lord.

Y'all, I would have been bawling my eyes out, ugly crying while squeaking out the words, "G... G... GOD, I... I... I... ttttrust Youuuuuuu, I TRUST YOUUUUU!"

Can you imagine how proud the Father was of her? I bet He even wept with her, knowing her heart was broken. Jesus weeps with us and cares about what hurts our hearts (John 11:35). When Jochebed birthed Moses, she may have seen destiny in his eyes and saw him as beautiful, yet three months later as she floated baby Moses into the midst of the reeds, I doubt she fully knew that he would grow up to be "a friend of God" or that he would lead the Hebrew people—her people—from slavery into freedom. I'm sure as his mother, she had a sense of great destiny over his life, but in that moment, she just knew she was having to give up her precious baby boy.

When we release fear and instead choose to trust God, stepping into the place of blind faith, greater dreams can be fulfilled. Sometimes we are right at the brink of greater freedom if we would only face our fears, let go, and step into trust. We may not always understand the letting go in the moment, but as we step into trust, we will see that His plan is greater and is *always* better. We need a faith that chooses to take risks, chooses to step into mustard seed faith and trust. We need a faith that through the trust, leaps into the will of God. We need a faith without walls, a faith without boundaries that's willing to release the most precious thing we hold onto, daring to let it go into the midst of the reeds and say, "God, I choose to trust You!"

Sometimes we are right at the brink of greater freedom if we would only face our fears, let go, and step into trust.

I think it's safe to say that God is not going to ask us to float our babies into a river with crocodiles, but sometimes He does ask us to hold loosely the things we deem so precious. Has God been speaking to you about trusting Him more? What are you afraid of? What are you holding onto so tightly that you are having a hard time letting go and trusting God with? Just like I believe He did with Jochebed, I believe God is saying,

"Don't be afraid. Will you trust Me and let go?"

Prayer of Trust

Father God,
I choose You! I choose to trust You.
I choose to let go of all the fears, the worries, the doubts,
and the lack of trust which keeps me from faith in You and Your goodness attached to _________ (fill in the blank and put whatever fear, worry, or doubt, etc., you are dealing with).
I give it to You and I choose to trust You.
I choose to believe that You are a good, good Father
who cares about my life, my heart, and all the issues surrounding it.
Today, I take a leap of faith and release _________ (fill in the blank) to You, and I choose to let it go because I know You love me.
I choose to believe You care about every detail of my life.
I love You, and I choose to take my mustard seed faith, let go, leave fear, and step into trusting You.
Amen.

Chapter 6

Why Not? Overcoming The Fear Of Man

Why not let go of fear? Why not step into faith and choose to trust? Can you be like Jochebed and punch fear in the face, choosing not to bow to man's ways and listen to the heart of the Father instead, clinging only to Jesus? Yes, I believe you can! Why not choose to trust Him? I did, and so can you.

If you are still reading this book, then I believe this is your season for breakthrough! Trust is a choice. When we feel powerless, we are choosing to not trust. Powerlessness says, "I can't," but the truth is, being a powerful person says, "I can, so why not!"

The Bible says in Philippians 4:13,

I can do all things through Christ who strengthens me.

We can't do it on our own. What keeps us from the *why not* is lack of trust, which as I've previously stated, is usually rooted in fear.

Maybe you prayed that prayer at the end of the last chapter, but you are still struggling. Let me ask you this:

What is holding you back, and what are you afraid of?

The truth is, the very things we are afraid to step out in are usually the very God dreams in our heart. God is waiting for us to trust Him with these dreams so He can partner with us to bring His Kingdom here to earth. I know that going through all I went through with my upbringing steeped in abuse—mentally, physically, sexually, and emotionally—kept me from fully trusting myself or trusting God in me. For many years, it kept me bound in fear instead of stepping into faith. I struggled with the fear of man, and in all honesty, at times it still tries to creep in. Even fear about writing this book and putting it out there for the world to read has tried to creep in. It felt scary and vulnerable. I realized elements of fear are still in me that have to die. Maybe you still struggle too. You are not alone.

What exactly is the fear of man? I want to address it because many will say, "I'm not afraid of people," yet internally they are terrified to step out into their greatness. They have deep rooted fear around what people will say or what people will think.

I really want you to lean in right now, and read this next part with an open heart. Ask Jesus, "Is any of this me?" If it is, don't feel shame. When God brings things to our attention, it's an opportunity for us to run at our Goliaths and lean into all that Jesus wants to do in us. Our end goal is freedom, and you will only find it in *the more* of Him. There is always more!

So, what holds us back? What holds *you* back? Could it be some of the things I mention below in the descriptions of the fear of man? Have an open heart, and with Jesus, read some of the definitions of the fear of man below.

FEAR OF MAN

1 – Definition

Fear of man is defined as an epidemic of the soul that can be characterized by peer-pressure, worry, and codependency. It is the act of placing others before God in one's life.

2 – Biblical Perspective

Fear of man is expressed biblically as a "snare" in Proverbs 29:25. In the book *When People Are Big and God Is Small*, Edward Welch best describes fear of man as,

> *"Fear in the biblical sense ... includes being afraid of someone, but it extends to holding someone in awe, being controlled or mastered by people, worshipping other people, putting your trust in people, or needing people."*

This isn't a small problem; it's a real struggle worldwide. In our human nature, the fear of man always tries to creep in and keep us bound. It's not something that can be dealt with in a flippant kind of way. It can only be met with the truth of God's Word. Scripture directs us to fear God rather than man. His Word through the Holy Spirit will lead you and guide you into all truth; He is our true comfort and the greatest truth teller.

Fear of man kept me in a snare for years. I struggled with stepping into trust and complete dependency on God, which I needed to do in order to step into greater faith. I personally didn't even trust *myself*. I mentally suffered with so much negative self-talk going on in my head and a heavy spirit of self-condemnation and comparison. I was afraid to step out, I was afraid to let my voice be heard, I was afraid of criticism, I was afraid of not being good enough, and to top it off, I was totally afraid of rejection. Other things that kept me bound like a prisoner in my own head were the following fears:

FAILING AND FAILURE

I hated to fail or feel like I was failing others. Because of that, it took me until I was in my late 40's to finally step into writing my first book—this book you're holding in your hands now. The truth is, failing isn't bad; it doesn't define who you are or who you feel you are called to be. We all fail at different points and seasons of our lives. To fail is to be human, and in reality, failure usually happens on the way to accomplishing our goals. When I casually typed this question on my computer—How many times do business people usually fail before they become successful—here's what came up:

"One in four entrepreneurs fail at least once before succeeding. It takes entrepreneurs an average of three years for their business to begin supporting them financially."

Failure is all about perspective. We need to have the perspective that when we fail it's teaching us something...so I like to choose to say *I'm failing forward*! We need to celebrate the progress we make in life, not the perfection.

We need to celebrate the progress we make in life, not the perfection.

BEING PERCEIVED AS WEAK

When I was in grade school, being called on was terrifying. If my teacher even looked at me and I thought she was going to ask me to answer a question, I would swallow hard as a lump formed in my throat, and I would have to fight back tears. Answering questions felt vulnerable. What if I got it wrong? Then, I would look stupid, and that just made me look weak and feel weak!

This was my train of thought. In my mind and heart, I genuinely believed that weakness was a sign of being really stupid. At home I repeatedly heard how stupid my ideas were or that something I did was stupid. I never wanted to be perceived as stupid. That played into my adult years and fueled the fire of the fear of man in my life.

BEING IRRELEVANT

This was a big one for me as well. Internally, I often felt lonely and forgotten as a child. I was third down the line in a family of six kids. I always tried to make people smile and feel comfortable, and I was the peacemaker. However, I was one of the quieter ones, especially in front of people I didn't know. As I mentioned in previous chapters, I suffered a lot of trauma as a child, and that really did a number on my mind and heart. I often felt like what I had to say didn't seem relevant and my opinions didn't really matter. "Shut up, do as I say or else" was what seemed like the strong hand of control that was consistently over my life. As I grew older, I was always afraid to step out, because *who would listen to what I have to say, it's not good enough, and my words and I are just not important enough*...or so I thought.

In January 2023, my sister Selina passed away. She was always the one who seemed like the life and soul of the party, with a vibrant and vivacious personality. She had a powerful set of lungs and could really sing! You would never guess she struggled with the fear of man because of the way she would take the mic or how she would walk right up to you with her hand extended and say, "Hi, my name is Selina. Who are you?" or, "Hello, I'm Selina. You don't know me yet, but you will!" She was only 49 when she passed away.

By the end of her life, she had never fully stepped into her greatness because of fear and the fear of man that she was steeped in.

My sister hid behind her vibrant personality. She had *a need to be liked.* She needed and desired man's approval, and she feared disapproval. I, too, had a need to be liked, so I hid behind a mask of trying to be perfect. One of the things I did that *supposedly* made me look perfect to others was to excel in my grades in the hopes of being praised. Can you relate to this?

My sister also had a *need for acceptance*. She always wanted to be the life of the party and be accepted wherever she went. She relished the praises of her friends and church people, especially when she would sing. I, too, had a need for acceptance, so I made sure to follow all the rules and always be the good girl—never the bad girl. I was so good that as I got older, some of my friends' parents would only allow their kids to go out or stay out late if they knew they were going out with me. I was known as the "goody two shoes." Does this resonate with you?

Selina suffered from *peer-pressure*. In high school, and sometimes in her adult life, she went the way of her friends, which resulted in partying, drinking, smoking, and having boyfriends she really shouldn't have had. She did all of it because she was looking to fill an aching void in her heart—a deep desire to simply feel loved. Like me, she was fatherless and also didn't have a mother who was very present. She was doing things she shouldn't have been doing and mixing with the wrong crowds on many occasions. She stayed in this place of always being a follower. Even though she had a loud voice and could be bossy, she never fully stepped into the place of being a true leader, and she had leadership ability. A victim mindset caused her to not take responsibility to care for herself or her body which, in turn, led her to suffer from diabetes and various other health issues. These were the sad results of the trauma she went through, her lack of belief in herself, and her lack of love for herself. Have you felt the squeeze of this in your life in one way or another?

Maybe like me you didn't smoke, you didn't party, drink, or do drugs, but maybe you have thrown yourself into your work or your church to find recognition to fulfill a need or a place of false identity. I know I did. Just like my sister, we all have *a need for recognition*. I call it the *look at me* syndrome. She needed to be noticed and seen. Her voice drew attention to herself all the time, as her lungs were really something. When my sister would walk into a room, you often knew she was there because she was loud! *"Selina has arrived! Look at me* was what her presence demanded. Can you relate?

I would give anything to hear her loud voice again, hug her neck, and be around her vivacious personality just one more time. We shared a room for most of our childhood years, and as much as she drove me crazy, I hid behind her loud, in-your-face personality. Some people would say it was her "ghetto" personality! At times, somehow, who she was made me feel safe in a funny sort of way. I didn't realize until I was an adult, and started to go through healing myself, how a lot of her loud and boisterous personality was a mask for what was really going on inside her heart.

I miss her, and I'm sad that she never fully got to live her life because of fear. She never trusted herself enough to step into her mustard seed of faith. The reality that *God really has me, I CAN trust Him,* and *only He can make all things work together for my good* wasn't there. She would say those things, but she didn't fully believe them.

The fear of man at one point or another has had, or still has, its claws in all of us. Now, you may still be thinking, *I don't think that I have or deal with the fear of man.* Maybe you don't, but maybe you do. The truth is, at one point or another, we all deal with this ugly enemy. It shows itself in different ways and in different personalities, but no matter how it displays itself, many times it's hidden from us. We don't recognize it. I want you to think about what I mentioned above—the different ways my sister and I suffered with the fear of man—and I want to invite you to also take a look at the symptoms on the following list. Read through it with the Holy Spirit and see what stands out to you.

SYMPTOMS OF THE FEAR OF MAN

- You second-guess your decisions.
- You measure your worth by compliments or criticism.
- You avoid speaking truth to prevent potential conflict.
- You struggle to say *no* for fear of disappointing people.
- You replay conversations in your head, worrying if you offended someone.
- You feel anxious when someone disapproves of you.
- You become timid when you should be bold.
- You become very bold, keeping your weaknesses from being seen.
- You judge your self-worth by other people.
- You are inactive/passive/procrastinate.
- You are not yourself around people.
- You are indecisive.
- You have unstable faith.
- You often think people don't like you.
- You avoid stepping out and taking risks to protect your reputation in case you fail.
- You hesitate to lead because you fear others' opinions.

What symptoms or aspects of the fear of man from that list resonate the most with you? Every single one of those were on my list at one point or another, so I encourage you not to partner with shame. Instead, partner with Holy Spirit as He walks you into freedom and healing.

I want to invite you into a time of healing now that you've identified areas that resonate with you. All of these aspects of the fear of man stem from somewhere, and I like to call those places *open doors*, which I've already mentioned in previous chapters. Yes, open doors are a real thing. Everything has a point of entry into your heart and life, either caused by you and your choices or because of something you walked through that wasn't necessarily your fault.

What are you allowing in? For me, many of the internal open doors were from my childhood. Your open doors may also be from childhood wounds—like negative words spoken over you, something done to you, something you walked through in your grade-school or high school, your work place, in a church setting with certain leaders over you, a bad business deal, a failed diet, a car crash, a bad college experience, etc. The list could go on and on.

An open door usually remains because of lies. We believe lies because of things we have walked through or what we were exposed to. Choosing to keep believing the lies leaves the door open for the enemy to gain access to our lives even more. Once we start believing lies, we begin to act on them, or rather *operate* in that mode. Proverbs 23:7 says,

As a man thinks, so is he.

The truth of the matter is, the body will go where the mind goes. If you feel triggered right now, I want to ask you to be brave and lean in. Jesus wants to come in, meet you right where you are, and bring healing. Just know that right now in this very moment, Jesus is near. Psalm 34:18 says Jesus is near to the broken hearted. God is for you. He desires for you to be free and to be living life to your fullest potential—even more than you desire it.

We are capable to step into our full potential. Why? Because God designed our hearts to operate at full capacity, stewarding the fullness of who we are. You are His perfect design whether you feel it, know it, believe it or not! When we have emotional pain attached to lies, we can't fully embrace the fullness of who we are or operate in the fullness of who we are called to be. Through some rough valleys in my life, what I have discovered is that our pain and the lies the enemy keeps bombarding us with are usually directly related to our giftings and what we were created for. He targets your destiny. He is scared that you will begin to discover your super powers in Christ Jesus. Yes, you are powerful!

We are capable to step into our full potential because God designed our hearts to operate at full capacity, stewarding the fullness of who we are.

When it comes to healing the heart, there is a divine exchange that happens when you let go and truly allow God to take the pain and the lies. You are anointed to do this because His Spirit is upon you! Take a moment and read out loud the following verses from Isaiah. Speak it out, declare it out loud, and breathe in the truth of this over yourself!

Isaiah 61:1–3 says;

The Spirit of the Lord GOD is upon me,
Because the LORD has anointed me to bring good news to the afflicted; He has sent me to bind up the brokenhearted,

to proclaim liberty to captives and freedom to prisoners;
To proclaim the favorable year of the Lord *and the day of vengeance of our God;*
To comfort all who mourn,
To grant those who mourn in Zion, giving them a garland instead of ashes, The oil of gladness instead of mourning, the mantle of praise instead of a spirit of fainting.
So, they will be called oaks of righteousness, the planting of the Lord*, that He may be glorified."*

What is the truth in this? It's that the Spirit of the Lord is upon you! He has anointed you! Why do you think the enemy has continuously tried to keep you from breakthrough, from trusting yourself, trusting God, and trusting others? It's because he is very, *very* afraid of who you are.

You see, before the foundations of the world were created, God knew you. Your life is powerful because of what you carry and Who you carry! There's power when you step into the fullness of trusting yourself, trusting Jesus, and trusting Him in you. That's why I keep driving this point. Going after the lies in our hearts and minds that imprison our gifts, our talents, and the truths of who we are is vital.

One of the things the enemy has gone after over and over again in my own life is *my voice*. In my head, I would even think my voice sounded funny. It didn't matter what I had to say, because why would people even care? Many times, after I spoke in front of people or from a platform I would feel like my voice was too much or wasn't good enough. But the truth is, every time I speak and minister, whether here in the USA or in the nations, people get radically touched and set free. It took years to finally step into trusting the truth and owning the fact that God is for me, that He wants to use my voice, and in Him *I am powerful* and *I am enough*! He gave me my gifts; therefore, I can trust Him and step out in faith.

Now, I'm finally confident that God wants to use my voice. I don't say this arrogantly; I say it with humble confidence, as I now know my identity isn't in my voice or what I do. My identity is simply found in being a daughter of the King. My Dad is my King, my Heavenly Father, and He is pretty amazing! I love that I get to be His daughter, and out of this relationship comes the overflow of what I do. As His daughter, I get to be a wife, a mother, a minister, a life coach, a mentor to students, a writer, a podcaster, and so much more. Ministering from this place of sonship is my passion. When you live life from sonship, you bring freedom to those around you.

When I minister and pray for people, I can often see in the spirit realm (as well as in the natural realm) the moment when people begin to get set free. Often times, there's an obvious shift in the person or in the crowd. I've seen tears start to flow and *aha* moments, when a light bulb of understanding and breakthrough sparks, and faces light up. On occasion, great joy comes on a person, usually followed by laughter they cannot contain.

This is an incredible privilege and a beautiful joy to see breakthrough happen for someone and to witness the emotional pain that sometimes has been bottled up for years be released. What a delight and an honor to watch them be healed in a single moment in the presence of God. Why is it so powerful? Because the person chose to take their mustard seed faith and step into trusting Jesus with their heart. They had faith to believe for the breakthrough from the trauma and all the lies.

As you have a learned, the enemy works strategically in our lives to keep us bound in lies, keeping us from sonship, and in doing so, shuts down our purpose on this earth. When we become aware of bound-up areas in our life, it is *essential* to break the strongholds that have been formed and renounce the lies we've believed.

RENOUNCING THE LIES

You may have gotten through some of the other chapters in this book and didn't feel the need to pray or renounce anything or shut any doors. But now, after reading this, you may realize there are things like fear and/or the fear of man that have crept into your mind. I want to challenge you to go after them with me.

Are you ready? Do you want freedom?

Take a moment, and find a quiet place where you can hear yourself think. It's time to write again. Sit with a pen, and using the space below or on a separate paper, write out any lies or fears that come to your mind.

____

____

____

____

____

____

Ungodly and unhealthy fears are wrapped up in lies. As I sat with the Lord and did this exercise myself, one of the things I wrote out was, "My voice is too much." When you hear things that are the opposite of God's truth, they are lies. Do this exercise with Holy Spirit; keep leaning in and keep writing out any lies the Holy Spirit shows you.

Now, one by one, let's renounce those lies. For me, I said something like this:

"I speak to the lie that says *my voice is too much*, and I break and sever all ties with this lie, in Jesus' name. Jesus/Lord/Father God, what truth do You want to give me in place of the lie that says my voice is too much?"

Now, sit with Him in this space, listen, and let Him speak. Take time to write out what you hear Him speak to you. You may not hear Him speak or think you don't, but God is always speaking, and maybe you hear or see more. You might see an image in your mind. If so, write it down or a memory of past moments. The truth always comes, so let Him speak how He wants to speak and write it out.

____

____

____

____

____

____

____

____

For me He spoke, "Mary your voice is powerful. I created it to bring breakthrough and healing for the nations."

So, in turn, I used the truth He spoke over me. I said out loud and declared,

"Jesus, I thank You and receive the truth over myself that my voice is powerful and You created it to bring breakthrough and healing for the nations. Thank you that You gave me my voice, that it is powerful, and that as I step out with You, my voice brings breakthrough and healing to many people around the world in the nations!"

I then turned that truth into a declaration that I spoke over myself and still speak it over myself:

"My voice is powerful. God created it to bring breakthrough and healing for the nations as I step out and trust Him."

As you begin to go after the lies and fill yourself with our Heavenly Father's truths over you, you'll begin to feel lighter and see things through the eyes of the Father. This isn't a one-time-fix-all type of thing either. As I have mentioned before, sometimes the very next day, the enemy will come back knocking and subtly bring thoughts like, *Is my voice really powerful? Am I really free? Will this really work?*

When he shows up, declare the truth again, stand your ground, and keep at the forefront of your mind that your place is to remember *you are powerful* even if you don't feel it! Step into that place, and tell him where to go back to. Tell him that he can go to hell and can take that lie with him. I love what Lisa Bevere once said when she was speaking at my church. She said, *"Hell isn't a cuss word, it's a destination."* Isn't that the truth! Get rightfully mad at the devil, and tell him to, "Go to hell!"

What I am giving you, friend, are tools to use daily, weekly, monthly, and yearly. There's no time limit or expiration for these tools, so use them as often as you need to. You are powerful to overcome because Jesus in you makes you powerful. You can do *all things* through Christ who gives you strength (Philippians 4:13), and you can trust Him!

I leaned into my mustard seed faith, and breakthrough began to happen. I began to trust God little by little with one area of my heart, then another and another until the breakthrough spread to every area. Everything is an invitation into greater intimacy. It's an invitation into greater adventures with the Father too, and guess what? They don't have to be hard. When you lean in, healing begins to take place and you find yourself smiling more. Fun, joy, and laughter can't help but happen around you, and wildly enough, you'll realize you are on a great adventure.

Chapter 7

International Adventures Of Faith With God

Being His daughter and living in Sonship is truly a great adventure. God really is fun. He really is so faithful and trustworthy. It's beautiful when you step into mustard seed faith and powerful when you see trust rise and greater faith grow. It's in this place where you begin to hope again. Stepping into a place of trust is one of the most powerful and rewarding things you can do. Choosing to step into it with Him is a key that can unlock the dreams of your heart. For me, it unlocked the nations.

When I began my journey of forgiveness, letting go, and breaking off the fear of man, God began to fill my heart with greater love and began to solidify my heart for missions. From the time I was little, going to the nations has been in my heart. I can remember as a little girl seeing the African babies on TV with bloated bellies and saying, "One day, I want to go there." As I got older, especially in my college years, my heart would ache for them. Way back then, the different people groups of this world were calling out to me, and the enemy tried to distort, steal it, and kill that call. However, he didn't win. The call is still going strong in my heart to this day, and it has taken me into many foreign countries and onto lots of great adventures with Jesus.

MEXICO

My first adventure in the nations was when I was 15 in 1991. I was already on my journey of healing, but the only person I had ever opened up to at this point in my life was my Beth (who I spoke of in chapter four). The abuse and traumatic childhood I had experienced were never discussed with outsiders in my world up to that point.

I kept myself involved in the youth group at my church, and even though I had frustration toward God, church was my place of escape, as was Beth and Bill's house. In these places, I could escape the loneliness I was feeling because of the love I felt when I was there. Also, I could escape the constant unsafe feeling and get away from the intense, oppressive environment my homelife carried.

Being my 15-year-old self, I immersed myself into the worlds outside of my home...really anywhere I could escape to. Being home hurt too much. Always looking for ways out, when the chance to go on a mission trip with my youth group to Mexico came up, naturally I jumped at the opportunity. It wasn't so much because my heart in this season of my life was fully sold out for missions yet; escaping my home life for one or two weeks was appealing.

Several buses full of young people from my church and others in Northern California and Nevada District were on this trip to Mexico. My group was dropped off near Tijuana at a little church with a tin roof. It looked more like an oversized shack.

On the first day, my group was approached by one of the translators—one of the church leaders there. We were told we would have nightly services to maximize our time so we could pour into the people. Each of us would be given an opportunity to share a testimony. She later turned to me and said, “Mary, you will give your testimony on the last night in the evening service!” I was floored and immediately piped up. “I don’t have a testimony; I was raised in a Christian home my whole life. I don’t want to share!”

I was mortified at the thought of having to speak in public, let alone share a testimony. The translator didn’t know that though. When she was done talking, I walked away and thought, *Phewww, I’m off the hook!* She found me later and pointed her finger in my face. “Mary, I KNOW you have a testimony and it’s something that’s hurt you deeply, and people need to hear it. God is going to bring it out of you before this week is over,” she said then turned and walked away.

It instantly felt like a knife went into my heart and twisted as she spoke those words. How did she know? I was shocked and mad. I just knew I couldn’t share; the thought of sharing felt too painful. *How could I possibly share about the physical abuse, the sexual abuse, and lay my heart bare before people I didn’t even know—people who had never gained my trust?*

Remember, the only person I had shared any of my story with up to this point was my Beth...*in private*! I wrestled with God, begging Him to help get me out of this. All week I wrestled with it, and then Friday finally came. Another girl and I were scheduled to sing a song in Spanish: “Él es mi paz—He is my Peace.”

The words to the first part of that song speak of how God is our peace and how we’re able to cast all of our cares on Him because He cares for us.

The song was so fitting for what was about to happen. I had no idea how God was about to break in and take over that night. So, although my singing wasn't perfect, it was something I could do. It made me very nervous, but it wasn't too hard because nobody knew me there anyway.

Speaking about what happened to me though...that was something altogether different, and it felt excruciatingly hard. The thought of it made me literally feel nauseous. My stomach hurt, and for a brief moment between the cold sweats, I thought I was going to throw up. Shame started creeping in, and it felt extremely painful. The other girl and I got through the song, and then she stepped off the little stage, leaving me standing there all alone.

With fear and trembling, I lifted the microphone and opened my mouth. Suddenly, a flood gate unlocked. God took over, and through a translator, as I shared, something started to happen. People started crying, and the whole time I was sharing, it felt like I was talking specifically to one young girl in the audience. When I finished and stepped off the little stage, it felt like a 1,000-pound weight lifted off of me. Somehow the world around me even seemed brighter.

Right away, the pastor took the microphone from me. Through the translator he said, *"We've heard the sermon for tonight. This is the Lord,"* and he immediately gave an altar call. That one girl I felt drawn to while speaking came running down the aisle and flung herself into my arms and cried and cried. I couldn't speak Spanish, but I could wrap my arms around her and hold her, feeling her hot tears roll off her cheeks onto my neck. I just cried with her. I held her as she and I wept.

Although I had no idea why she was weeping because of our language barrier, I knew it was deep pain, and I knew she was finding healing and freedom in that moment. People gave their lives to Jesus that night, and the service lasted until late in the evening. It was beautiful, wild, and crazy to see God crash in so powerfully.

The next day, as we were getting back on our bus to leave, I heard my name being called. "Mary, Maria, Mary!" I looked out the window to see the translator who had told me that I had a testimony and God was going to bring it out of me before the week was over. She was running alongside the bus trying to find me. I stuck my head out the window to signal her. She came on the bus and proceeded to tell me all about the young girl who ran to the altar and flung herself into my arms. She relayed to me how that young girl was only 17 and was pregnant with her stepfather's baby. She had told her mother about it but was scoffed at; her own mother didn't believe her. Her mother told her, "You're only whoring around with the boys in the neighborhood," and was getting ready to kick her out of the house.

Then, the translator proceeded to tell me how the girl was so undone by Jesus and said, "If Mary could go through all that she went through, then I know God has His hand on my life, and I want to give my life to Jesus tonight." When I heard that, I was broken and started to cry. As tears ran down my face, my heart leapt with joy. My heart was over the moon!

I couldn't help but rejoice that day on the long bus ride back to the Bay Area of California. The ride to Mexico felt like it took forever, but the ride back didn't seem so long this time. My heart was captivated and undone by the Father. As I contemplated my week and all God had done, I knew my life would never be the same.

As we made the journey home, I purposed in my heart and told the Lord, God, if I went through all the abuse that I went through so that You, through me, could touch that one life, then it was worth it all. I never got to see that girl again or what happened to her baby, but I made a promise to God: God, I will never hide my story again when You ask me to share.

God, if I went through all the abuse I went through so that You, through me, could touch that one life, then it was worth it all.

You know, there is something about sharing your testimony publicly that brings you into another realm of breakthrough. It causes the enemy to fear you, and it causes him to have to loosen and sometimes completely let go of his grip on you and your voice.

The Bible says this in Revelation 12:11:

And they overcame him because of the blood of the Lamb and because of the word of their testimony...!

Even in your pain, when you choose to be brave and step out into your mustard seed faith, trusting that God is good and has your best interest in mind, it creates worlds of greater breakthrough for you and others. Your stories of breakthrough matter. Nobody can take them away from you, and nobody can tell them quite like you.

Over the years, I've only shared this story from Mexico when God prompts me to. However, I feel more and more compelled that it's time to let the truth of my story be heard loud and clear. Who is waiting for you to step up and step out? I believe there are people all around you and potentially even in the nations of this world waiting specifically for you to open your mouth, and when you do, their freedom will be right around the corner. When you step out in faith and choose to do life with Jesus, greater freedom always comes, and you never know what adventures He will take you on.

ISRAEL

After I graduated high school in 1995, the opportunity came for me to go to Israel on another mission trip. The difference this time was that I wasn't running away from my home life. This time, I was adventuring with Jesus and felt compelled to the nations.

I needed just over $3,000 for the trip, so I sent out fundraising letters. People in the church donated, but I still didn't have enough money, and the financial deadline was getting down to the wire. One day before the last payment was due, I still needed another $500. I kept putting the need before God. God, I have no idea where the money will come from, but I know You called me to go on this trip.

It was a Sunday night, and I was at my evening church service. Afterward, a stranger walked up to me and said God had told them to give me a check. I graciously received it, and to my excitement, it was the full $500 that I needed to pay off the trip. God surprised me! He is always so faithful.

The departure day came, and our group boarded our plane for Israel. The flight felt long, as I had never been on an international flight like this, but it was mesmerizing. I saw Jews get up to pray at the back of the plane, complete with prayer shawls over their heads and wearing Tefillin (the black leather strap they wrap seven times around their arm). I didn't want to stare at them as they prayed rocking back and forth, but I caught myself glancing quickly many times as curiosity got the best of me.

> I was in awe of God's faithfulness and excited to be in the land where Jesus was raised.

About 14 or 15 hours later, we landed in Tel Aviv. I was in awe of God's faithfulness, and being in the land Jesus was raised in was exciting. The day after we landed, we set out ministering from Tel

Aviv to Haifa, Acra, Nazareth, through the West Bank, Jericho, Bethlehem, and ultimately Jerusalem. We ministered in Messianic churches and on the streets, doing open air evangelism, giving our testimonies, doing dramas/skits about God, sharing His salvation message, and releasing the love of Jesus from person to person, going from one town to another.

Along the way we got to see, pray, worship, and read from the Bible at many of the biblical sites where Jesus went and where incredible things happened. We visited Simon the Tanner's house, where Peter had a vision of the sheet coming down from Heaven and saw that all things were made clean to eat (Acts 10:5–16). We also went to Cana, where Jesus performed His first miracle of turning water into wine (John 2:1–12). We got to pray at Golgotha, and as we prayed, the presence of God was so thick that it literally felt like Heaven came down. I believe it did in some ways, and in that moment, we were all weeping. One of my favorite places was the Mount of Olives in Jerusalem, where Jesus prayed in the Garden of Gethsemane (Matthew 26:36–46).

There was so much peace as we read from Scripture, and you could feel His presence all around. We traveled and would stop at these places to pray and sometimes minister there, but when we reached Jerusalem, you could tell there was a shift in the spiritual realm. I remember having to rely heavily in my trust in God that He would keep us safe, because I could feel fear trying to come on me.

During our last night in Jerusalem, we set up our speakers on the streets, inviting people to watch our drama of the creation story—about God's heart of love for His people. Right away, some rabbis in long black robes—I believe they were orthodox—were irate and didn't want us to minister. They were trying to tear down our portable sound system. Some of us were trying to hurriedly pass out Bibles to people who wanted them, and a little, old, hunched-back woman came up to me sweetly...or so I thought. Thinking she wanted a Bible, I handed her one, but her demeanor shifted. With squinted, piercing eyes that looked almost black, she said with a snarl and growl in her broken English, "NO YESHUA." Then, with what I perceived to be supernatural strength for a hunchbacked old woman, she proceeded to rip the paperback Bible in half.

No sooner had that happened, when suddenly we were being told to run and were being ushered through some passageways and underground tunnels to safety. To this day, I believe the people leading us to safety were potentially secret police or angels in human form because our lives were in danger. Regardless of the danger, God provided a way out.

God moved on that trip and in my life mightily as I stepped out and as I chose to trust Him and partner with Him through faith. Because of faith, we were able to plant seeds. God came through as my Provider and my Protector in tangible ways. Many people including myself were changed on that trip, and hundreds of people were saved and set free. God is so faithful!

CAMEROON, WEST-CENTRAL AFRICA

As someone who had a love for the nations in my heart since I was a child, my ultimate desire was to one day go to Africa. When I was little, I would see TV commercials of little orphaned kids of people with different ministries doing various projects like digging water wells in Africa, or people providing meals to poverty-stricken villages. I would listen to missionaries who visited my church from time to time and was drawn to the pictures of the little brown babies with bloated bellies, snot running down their noses, and flies around their eyes. Missions became my heartbeat as I could feel the Father's heart for the nations.

At the end of 1999, I was part of the Brownsville Revival and joined their School of Ministry based in Pensacola Florida. It was there where I had the opportunity to go on my first missions trip to Africa. I was beyond excited, but once again I had to believe God for the money to go. Again, I needed a little over $3,000 for the trip. God had provided for countless youth trips to snow camps, summer camps, the Mexico youth trip, and Israel, so, once again I found myself attaching high beliefs of faith that He was going to come through for this trip to Africa.

He didn't disappoint. He totally came through, and this time it happened fast. Within a few weeks, the money came in from various sources, like bonuses at my work and people who felt led to sow into me. More and more with each step of faith, I have grown to trust God in bigger ways; over and over I've realized my God is a God of abundance, and He lacks no good thing. There is no lack in Heaven, so I believe that when His children attach faith to the ask, He will provide!

Cameroon, at first, was pleasant and fascinating. The country was lush and beautiful. Once we landed, there was no mistaking we were on African soil. Everything just felt and smelled different. Upon leaving the airport, we were met by people selling things on the road, like dried bat on a stick (think beef jerky) and boiled peanuts in plastic bags. There were also lush green banana trees everywhere. Many of the roads were dirt, but many were paved as well...albeit with the biggest potholes I had ever seen. Let me tell you, needing back adjustments after driving or being a passenger in a car in many parts of Africa is so real. Chiropractors would make lots of money setting up practices in many parts of Africa if they could charge US prices.

Every day as a team, we went into the streets, set up our sound system, did evangelistic dramas, which would draw huge crowds, and we preached the Gospel. A couple of times while traveling via bus, we were stopped. Authorities would come onto our bus and demand for all of our passports to be given to them to be looked over. My heart always raced when this would happen because they always seemed rough. However, God kept His hand on us as we continued to travel and step out.

In every area and in just about every village, we saw people give their lives to Jesus. We saw healings take place, hopelessness break off of people, and witchcraft renounced. It was so powerful! Cameroon was also the country where I first encountered praying for resurrection life over a beautiful little African boy who had been dead for several days. The family had heard we were coming to their village and heard that our God can raise the dead.

A few of us were chosen on that rainy day to go with our leader up the side of this slippery, muddy mountainside to a little shack where this little boy lay. Upon arriving to his home, we found him laying on an old raggedy looking couch. He was perfect and beautiful in every way, except he looked ashen, and we were told he was dead. There was no breath in his lungs.

We prayed for what seemed like hours over him, and it seemed like all the eyes in the village peered through the cracks in the walls of that little tin-roofed shack. I was excited, and I knew if God would raise him from the dead, the whole village would come to life in Jesus Christ. I couldn't wait! My spirit leapt inside of me. I just knew this would be my Matthew 10:7–8 day. I truly believed it was going to happen; why wouldn't it?

We stood around his lifeless little body, prayed, and kept praying until finally we prayed no more. That precious little boy still laid lifeless, and my heart was sad and broken for the family. Suddenly, I found myself furious at God. I didn't have a grid for this, and I felt it unjust. God, why would You not raise him from the dead? Especially when You tell us to ask anything in Your name? He even commands us in the Bible to raise the dead. In John 14:14, He says to ask anything in His name and He will do it. But in that moment, He didn't. I held that in my heart the rest of the trip.

The plane ride back to the USA felt exceptionally long, and I told myself that I never wanted to go back to Africa ever again because of how hard it was. There were many variables, but one of the big ones was that it felt sad and hard because of the lack of resurrection. Pain from other disappointments and hardships on that trip lingered as well. My heart was broken as I built a case against Africa and God in my heart and mind, wrestling with the famous question, "Why, God?"

I never fully got my answer to the whys, but sometimes faith looks like what we talked about before:, stepping into trust to forgive, letting go, and trusting that His ways are higher than ours, even when we don't know the why. Faith looks like ultimately trusting, that He sees the bigger picture more than we can, and it looks like leaning into Him even when we don't understand. Everything is an invitation into greater intimacy with God. He is not afraid of the hard, frustrated, or disappointed questions we ask Him. After

Everything is an invitation into greater intimacy with God.

all, He is truth, and His goal is relationship with us. He is after our hearts.

TANZANIA, EAST AFRICA

God is a God of redemption. Although I had sworn in my heart to never go back to Africa because Cameroon was so hard on me mentally, emotionally, and spiritually, He had other plans. In 2001, after completing ministry school, I found myself on staff at Fire School of Ministry in Pensacola, Florida, as the Dean of Women. Some of the leaders in the school were going to be leading a team to Tanzania. When I found this out, my heart leapt, and I really didn't expect that. To my surprise, Africa was still in my heart, and although I was a bit fearful, I still found myself aching to go back. God was still stirring my heart.

He had given me space after Cameroon, and I came to a conclusion: You, God, are still good, and I choose to trust You (remember, it's a choice). Once again, I stepped into this place of faith, praying and asking God to show up and provide financially for this trip. As I stepped out in faith, God stepped in. He provided all of the money, a little over $2,500, within a few short weeks. I was so excited, and something felt different this time. My heart had been given enough time to heal as I leaned into disappointment from my first trip to Africa, and I had allowed myself time and space to process it with the Lord.

I will never forget arriving in Tanzania. The plane hit the ground on the tarmac runway in a perfect touchdown landing. I gathered my carry on and started to make my way down the aisle to disembark. Nervous but also excited, the huge KLM jetliner's doors opened, and I made my way down the big stairs onto the concrete runway. A smokey smell hung in the air, and even though it was nighttime and the rainy season, the East African sun's heat from the day hit my face. I couldn't put my finger on it as to why, yet somehow in my spirit this trip just felt different.

On this trip, I took everything in, including the sounds. The mosque's call to prayer at 5 a.m., the roosters crowing in the wee hours of the morning, the loud bush baby lemurs, the bats screeching at night, fighting over the zambarau fruit, and the crickets and frogs filled the night hours with a rich orchestra of unique sounds.

Daily, we ministered in churches. We spent time growing friendships, and the Tanzanian people were so friendly and inviting. Right away, my heart was drawn in, and on day three when I was speaking in one of our evening revival services, I found myself saying, "I will be back here full-time!" In the depths of my heart I knew God was calling me full-time to this foreign land of beauty, and I wasn't holding back; the world had to know.

This trip to Tanzania was pivotal. My yes to Jesus as I stepped out in faith that night, declaring my return, created a world of future and promise over my life. By June of 2003, I had made my way back to Tanzania, and the only difference this time was I was going as a full-time, 27-year-old, single missionary woman. I was living a life of full devotion to Jesus, helping in orphanages, helping with a church plant, teaching in our small Bible school, leading a worship team, leading a drama evangelism team, and getting to speak at women's conferences here and there. I was about my Father's business and had no grid for what was about to happen in my life.

It was in Tanzania in 2003 where I would find myself attending a small worship gathering at the home of seasoned missionaries Steve and Anne Street. They would host worship nights where missionaries and other foreign believers in our area would gather, and this was where I would later meet my husband Peter, who was their middle son. He was a missionary kid born in Scotland but was raised in Tanzania from age five on. Our relationship began as friends. I would give him dating advice, and we'd have long conversations. We enjoyed each other's company, and somewhere along the way, it was like a light bulb came on. We began to realize we liked each other, but we didn't actually start to date until 2006. It was an on again and off again relationship, even breaking off our engagement, which was due to mainly my fear and both of our need for growth.

God worked a lot on both of us, and in July 2007, we got married (7-7-07). It was truly a full circle moment in our lives. A year later in 2008, my journey as a mother in the natural realm began, giving birth to our first daughter, Hope. In the midst of childhood pain, roads of uncertainty, journeys of forgiveness toward others, toward God and toward myself, hope has always been a consistent theme in my life. I was always drawn to that word. It was like my spirit deeply resonated with it, so naturally we named our first born just that...Hope!

As time went on, our family increased, having four more children: Faith, Asher (who I miscarried with), Naomi, and Luke. There is so much more I could share and write regarding my journey and the 16 years I spent in Tanzania. However, I know the majority of my life's story is for another book. Stay tuned for that.

Throughout my life, God has been a God of hope, even when I was angry at Him. In the pain, the hardships, and the disappointments, I could still feel and see glimmers of hope with each passing day, week, month, and year. As these stories of my international adventures with God have woven their way into a beautiful tapestry throughout my life, looking back I can very much see His faithfulness.

As I held onto hope, and chose to step into mustard seed faith, it truly unlocked trust, catapulting me into a greater, radical faith that many people will only ever read about. For many, it's hard to comprehend because they can't see or envision things as being possible. But they are possible, and if it's possible for me, it is for you too. Whether you are married or single, all of you have God adventures waiting for you, no matter what season you find yourself in.

Will you lean in with your mustard seed of faith, step into greater trust, and really allow the Father to lead you?

Chapter 8

Stepping Into Greater Trust And The 'I Do'

I've chosen to trust God because He is so trustworthy. His promises over us are good. Through the many adventures with God, I have seen Him come through as my Provider, Protector, my Lover, my Best Friend, and a good, good Father. I know I can trust Him.

If you would have asked me 22 or so years ago, I would have confessed to trusting Him, but my heart, at times, was far from it. As a single missionary living on the mission field, my life was adventurous. Although I loved it, there was one pain point for me: marriage. I really, really wanted to be married. Here I was at age 27, thinking I would have been married by that point in my life and sharing those adventures with my spouse. How would I ever find a husband who was willing to be in the nations with me? My faith dwindled, and at times, felt non-existent. Yet, in the midst of the pain of my situation, I refused to swear to a life of celibacy because my heart so longed to be married. At that age...let's face it, your hormones are raging. You want a husband to make love to and share your life with, but sometimes it felt far off and unattainable.

Throughout life, one of the greatest lessons I have learned is that God doesn't lead us astray or dangle an impossible carrot to reach in front of our face. Circumstances in our lives may feel like it sometimes. For me, marriage was one of those things. I trusted God in most areas of life, but not in all areas. When it came to commitment in romantic relationships, that was one of those areas in my heart that felt scary, because it involved a deeper level of trust and vulnerability.

As you can imagine, I never had the greatest view of marriage as a child. With my biological family's history, I knew divorce and I knew total submission to the man as the leader of the home, which left no room for a wife to truly become herself. In some ways, it felt like if your husband said, "Jump," then you as a wife needed to ask, "How high?" This was the picture that was painted for me: total submission in everyday marriage.

I saw nothing but pain wrapped around marriage until Beth and Bill came into my life. Their kind of marriage, however, felt unattainable—almost fairytale like. To strive for that kind of marriage felt like the unreachable dangling carrot, yet I wanted a marriage like theirs that felt secure. For me, divorce was never going to be an option. The "D" word was never going to be on the table, so there were high stakes to get it right the first time. Would it *ever* happen with my super-high standards?

These standards set the bar high, sometimes even to the point where it was realistically unattainable. There was a certain "type" of guy I was looking for, besides him being good looking. This type of guy I "needed" was, funnily enough, what others told me I "needed" or the type they saw me with. I knew I was headed into full-time ministry, primarily into missions, and I wanted someone who could preach, sing, play the piano and/or the guitar (which was a bonus), and he had to have a heart for missions. You know, the perfect church boy. Ha!

When I first went to what was known as "Central Bible College" in Springfield, Missouri, I was so sure I had found the right man, or rather, sure that he had found me. He came to me within the first few months of being there, saying he had seen me in a dream on that very campus before he had ever met me, and so he pursued me. Needless to say, we dated for almost a year. In my mind, of course he was *the one*. At the end of the year, we were both leaving for the summer back to our home states, so we decided to pause our relationship for the summer to define our relationship. We were pretty serious and really wanted to take time out to pray and see for sure where it was going and if it was what God wanted. We didn't speak over the summer and gave each other some space.

When the summer ended, I flew back to Springfield, Missouri, very excited to start the new school year. I had prayed and felt good about where the relationship was going. We all got back to campus, everyone buzzing as we stepped into the new season.

Once I arrived on the campus, some of my friends approached me right away. "Did you hear?" they asked. My stomach was in knots. Suddenly, I had a bad feeling. Sure enough, the devastating news came. I found out the hard way through the grapevine that he was engaged to *another* girl.

Wow! I was shocked and angry. *How dare he not even have the decency to be a man and tell me himself before I found out through others.* I was gutted. He was the perfect guy for me, or so I thought. He could preach, he could sing, he could play the piano, he had a heart for missions, and he helped lead CMF—the Campus Missions Fellowship for people who had a heart for missions to gather and seek God together. We were the couple that would pull the car over and dance in the rain. He would bring me flowers he had picked, and I wore his letterman jacket. In many people's eyes, and in mine, I really thought we were the perfect couple, until we weren't.

My heart was broken after that horrible betrayal. I was so mad at him and hurt. I was mad at myself for giving my heart away. I was mad at God for allowing me to be in that relationship, and I just didn't understand. God, in His lovingkindness, guides us, but as a good Father, He lets us make our own choices. He never wants robots; He desires sons and daughters. I'm so glad He allowed me to walk through that season because it was a growth season for me. It helped me realize packages may look perfect on the outside, but God sees the heart. Our relationship looked like a pretty package that would be tied up and delivered with a lovely bow on top. However, looking back, I know my heart wasn't truly ready. I needed more healing and more time to grow.

God in His lovingkindness guides us, but as a good Father, He lets us make our own choices.

It was during my time in college when I heard the Lord tell me that I would marry and I needed to trust Him. In this season of my young life, I had my list of what I wanted in a husband. I also had a list of the perfect plan: married by the time I was 21, my first baby by the time I was 25, and be on the mission field in some foreign land by the time I was 27. Do you notice the one theme in these statements? You guessed it...it was "I." God had a plan, but the ears of my heart were not listening. My eyes were focused on *my* plan not His.

I ended up going through several more relationships, enduring several more heartaches with great guys in my Bible college years and after, but they were not the right ones. I even ended up engaged to one of them, which truly tested my trust in the Lord yet again. I had stepped out and opened my heart to this other guy because I thought I heard the Lord say he was the one, and there were many "signs" that pointed to him being it, or so I thought. My trust in God, the trust I had in myself to make good decisions, and my faith was truly tested along the way. None of the guys I dated were bad...well, with the exception of maybe one or two. But all in all, to this day, most of the guys I dated are in some form of ministry within the church or on the mission field. One is working in the political arena in his city. Like I said, most were great, but they just were not the right one.

What's also really funny is that the guy I was briefly engaged to, his last name in French is the word street and I ended up marrying a Street. We've remained distant friends over the years, and he teased that back then, I was barking up the wrong *street*! At least we can laugh about it now, but at the time, it was an extremely hard break up. I questioned myself and God over and over again. Why did I keep missing it?

When it came to relationships, I had a hard time trusting myself and trusting God. It didn't help that divorce was a factor in my family, which made commitment feel scary. Knowing my calling was to the church, and particularly in foreign missions, I was afraid of missing the mark, afraid of choosing the wrong guy. After all, the wrong guy could take me away from God's "perfect plan" for my life, right? As much as my heart was broken, I, too, broke many hearts out of fear. More and more I questioned my ability to hear God well, and I didn't trust myself to make good relationship decisions. Even though

I thought I heard God say I would be married, the question rolling around in the back of my mind and at the forefront of my heart was, *Will I be single for the rest of my life?* I laid down the desire of my heart to be married on the altar hundreds of times, giving it to God through heavy, snot-filled tears, for years before it really happened.

As I said in the last chapter, at 27 years old, I chose to step full-time into what I believed to be my life's calling. I left for the mission field as a full-time missionary to Tanzania, Africa. Remember, I had asked God to let me be married by the time I was 21, and that didn't happen. I wanted to have my first baby by the time I was 25, and that didn't happen either. Out of the three *I's* that I wanted God to give me, the only thing that came to pass was heading to the mission field at age 27. Married or not, I choose to spread my wings and fly. I wanted to be on the mission field and never doubted this area of my life.

With no doubt God had spoken, there I was, single on the foreign mission field at age 27 with my biological clock ticking. I loved Africa. Everything in my heart felt fulfilled except for this one area, and I found myself grumbling, complaining, and questioning God. *Why, God? Why am I not married and here with my husband? Why does it have to be this way? I wasn't supposed to be here single and alone!* (Cue the many, many nightly tears.)

This was the cry of my heart. I wanted so badly to be married, not single, and I felt so alone. Yes, my biological clock was ticking, but it wasn't just about sex; I wanted to feel wanted and to have a true partner—a forever friend. I deeply desired a husband to love and make love to. I wanted to be held at night. I wanted to feel that kind of deep love and be loved deeply in return. I wanted children and a family to share this amazing life with. I cried myself to sleep many nights, tears drenching my pillow over and over again, as the ache in my heart grew bigger and bigger.

There was one song called "Worth It All" by Rita Springer who was a powerful Christian artist and worship leader in my younger years, and her song comforted me in this season. I would play this song on repeat day and night, sometimes until I fell asleep. I played it while pouring my heart out to God until I felt a shift in my mind and heart.

This was the path I chose, and I also knew God invited me to go and work in Africa in this season of my life. I really didn't understand the why or His ways in the midst of the pain of singleness, yet I felt God drawing me into a deeper place of peace and trust with Him. All I had to do was trust Him with my little mustard seed of faith.

In this season, my mustard seed of faith really began to grow roots deeper and deeper in new ways, and God was strengthening my foundation in Him. Little did I realize, God was already working on my behalf and preparing my future husband. He only needed me to take my little mustard seed of faith and step into trusting Him with the deepest desires of my heart.

Saying *yes* to Jesus and moving my life to Tanzania in 2003 was a huge leap of faith, and I had no idea I would meet my future husband Peter that same year. God already had a plan and was making all things work together for my good. He was already putting my greatest heart's desire in motion, getting ready to answer my heart's cry.

Peter wasn't the kind of guy I would have normally been interested in. As a matter of fact, when we first met, I wasn't really attracted to him and never thought twice about him in that way. I clearly remember the first night we met. As I mentioned in the previous chapter, Peter's parents were longstanding missionaries in

Moshi, Tanzania, and many of us knew them. It happened to be a worship night at their house (which they held regularly), and there was a group gathered there to worship as the body of Christ. It was so beautiful. This particular night, we were in the middle of worshiping when in walks Peter Street with a friend he had been backpacking with. Here was a tall, unkept looking, ruddy, blonde guy wearing shorts, an old t-shirt, and flipflops—not at all "my type." But he had a sweet smile and gorgeous, kind blue eyes.

After meeting that night, Peter was so easy to talk to, and we quickly became friends. He had a job as a water engineer. Working for a German company during this season, he would often travel out of the country. After our initial meeting, we only saw each other from time to time when he was in town. I always knew when he was back in town though, because I'd see him speeding by on his white and red dirt bike (in Swahili we say "pikipiki"). Of course, there he would be on his motorcycle in a t-shirt, shorts, and malapas (flipflops)—his signature style. And there I was every morning, exercising and on my usual walks, and he'd stop to greet me. We'd end up standing on the side of the road to chat. More and more, those chats became longer and longer, until they were eventually over an hour long on those Shanti Town Moshi roadsides at the base of Mt. Kilimanjaro.

The two of us would talk about life, his travels, church stuff, Jesus, and girls. Yes...I would give him dating advice while talking about God, life, and love. We were just friends. He would make me laugh and he was fun, but I never really gave it a second thought until...something shifted. After a while, my heart started to get excited to see him. I would find myself hoping he was in town and that he would come speeding by. I started to look forward to our roadside chats.

As time went on, with each chat, I found myself falling into his kind smile, his peaceful, fun-loving personality and baby-blue eyes. He carried such a sweetness, a gentleness, and genuine love for people, and I loved that about him. My missionary teammate, who also was my housemate at the time, would always tell me, "Mary Navarro (my maiden last name) whatever you do, do not fall for Peter Street." In her eyes, she probably thought he wasn't good enough for me and was being protective. I kept telling her not to worry and that I wouldn't. Ha! Little did I know, I very much would, and it would be so God and so worth it!

Peter and I began going on pikipiki (motorcycle) rides together, zipping up the mountainside of Mt. Kilimanjaro. I'd put on his extra motorbike helmet, hike my long skirt up (yes, that was my womanly missionary signature style at the time), jump on the back of the dirt bike, hold his waist, and off we'd ride. I secretly began to love getting to hold onto him, and it somehow felt right, yet I wouldn't let myself fully go there in my heart. Somewhere deep inside, I was still afraid of missing God's perfect best for me, and I was afraid of rejection too. Ultimately, I was afraid of choosing the wrong person.

Somewhere deep inside, I was still afraid of missing God's perfect best for me, and I was afraid of rejection too.

We were friends until the DTR day came. Remember, define the relationship (DTR)? Yup, that day came! I can remember as if it were yesterday. At this time, our team was preparing for a three-month internship team to come to Tanzania, which was made up of seven people from different US states. We still had some building and room painting preparations to do to get ready for the team before they arrived in a week, so I was in full work mode.

On one particular day, the team and I were working in a room, and I was up on a ladder, painting. I had no makeup on, and I was wearing a cutoff sleeved t-shirt, my hair was under a bandanna, and I was looking pretty hot...*not!* Let's just say I looked rough, not my usual put together self. All of a sudden, I hear the day guard open up the gate, and in zips Peter on his dirt bike. My heart started pounding. It was like I knew something was about to happen. Suddenly I felt so nervous with the very guy I would have long motorbike rides with and best friend conversations.

As soon as he parked, he came inside and stood there chatting with us, yet I could tell he was kind of nervous...which made me even *more* nervous. I started sweating at this point, and I couldn't figure out what was going on. He waited until the room cleared, and when it finally did, there we were, just the two of us. I was painting, looking really hot (*wink wink*), and he asked if he could talk to me. Yup, my heart was ready to bounce out of my chest. *Ahhhh, what is about to happen?*

I stood there on the ladder looking cool, calm, and collected and, so of course I obliged. He began to sweetly, yet a little shyly, open up his heart and share how he really felt about me. A million thoughts ran through my head as he talked and I painted. He stood there patiently, albeit a little nervous too, and proceeded to see if I was interested in actually dating. I nervously stayed at the top of the ladder, still painting the same spot over and over again. I'm pretty sure that spot ended up being darker than other areas!

After spilling out his heart, he waited for me to say something. What do you say in a moment like that when you have a million things swirling around in your mind and heart? I knew we were good friends at this point, but like I said, I was nervous. I can't say that enough...*I WAS NERVOUS*! Was this really happening? This could make or break our friendship. *Oh God, what do I say? What do I do?*

After a long pause, Peter asked, "Aren't you going to say anything?" I *wanted* to say something. However, the truth of the matter was I was scared. Could I really trust my heart? Could I trust his heart with mine? *What if I miss it again? What if he isn't "the one," and I ruin my whole life?* I truly believed I could ruin and throw away the plans of God over my whole life by making this one choice. (Let's just laugh at that lie—haha.) Could I trust God in this?

I remember slowly climbing down the ladder, keeping one foot on the last rung and planting my other foot firmly on the floor. One hand was on my waist, and the paint brush was in the other. I slowly turned my head toward him, looking him in the eyes, and began to open my mouth. WHOA! Out came a whole slew of *matter of facts* along the lines of...

"Well...Peter Jonathan Street, you need to know who I really am. I've had a call of God on my life for ministry and missions since I was little.

I've been through a lot of horrible things and trauma in my life, both physically and sexually. I've never really known my real dad, as my parents split when I was in the womb.

My family isn't glamourous. I know I'm called to missions and to Africa.

I am a revivalist through and through. My life was radically touched and changed in the fires of the Brownsville Revival. I have literally shaken for three days straight when the presence of God came on me, and I couldn't even talk. I'm not your average or ordinary woman.

I am called to preach and teach the Word of God. Sometimes God calls me away to be with Him for three days or more at a time. He is my everything! If (*SIGH*) you think you can handle a woman like me, then maybe you might have a chance!"

Phew...that was a mouthful. Can you even imagine the moment? As a guy who simply wanted to know if we could date, what must he have been thinking? He didn't run. He was still standing there. He had some guts! I won't give away any spoilers (I'll save that for another book), but I will say I was surprised when that didn't scare or visibly rattle him. Even though I have carried a lot of peace, I still exuberated authority and high leadership skills that often put off some of the guys I dated, to the point it felt like we were more in competition with one another instead of in a real relationship. Peter wasn't that kind of guy; he was different. He had confidence and an inner strength which was so attractive as we got to know each other more. After I spewed my heart, in that moment, he responded with,

"My family and I are headed to Mombasa, Kenya, for a week-long family holiday, so I'll have my mum and dad pray, and I want you to pray about it too. When I come back, let's talk."

Let me tell you, that week felt very long! I cried as I called out to God, wrestling and wrestling internally, asking Him over and over if this potential relationship was of Him. Spoiler alert, there had been another guy I was interested in as well, but he hadn't made any feelings for me known. All in all, I never had a great peace or lack thereof, and I never heard a "thus saith the Lord" or had that kind of epiphany moment. My heart was drawn to Peter, and so I leapt in.

When he came back from Mombasa, we started dating. It was a crazy time for me with this new relationship, juggling the internship I was co-leading, and navigating my heart to trust myself and trust God in this process. After many broken relationships with good guys, could I trust God in this? Could I trust that God was leading me? Could I trust that there wasn't someone or something better out there for me?

Peter was a great guy, but he didn't check all the boxes on my preconceived "husband" list. Didn't God want me to have *the best* and the ultimate desires of my heart? The internal wrestle continued.

We dated, and I broke up with Peter multiple times, even after we first got engaged. Many people would have thrown in the towel, saying, "If you don't have peace, just don't go there." But the truth was, my peace was squelched by my fear to step into trust. So, there I was, questioning everything. I questioned myself, my ability to believe and trust God, I questioned Peter's love for me and if he was God's best. What I was really doing was *running*. I was afraid, running from my own heart.

> I just didn't trust myself or trust God with this part of my life. I realized I had to break up with that lie.

Peter and I separated for six months at one point, and in those six months I came face to face with this fear within the depths of my heart. People always deemed me "the runaway bride," and in my heart of hearts, I subconsciously believed that. This was the one part of my life where I didn't trust myself or God. *Runaway bride...* I realized I had to break up with that lie. I *wasn't* a runaway bride. I had to face my fear of making a bad relationship choice and missing the call of God over my life. God began to speak to me about this, and one day as I was journaling, He spoke these words over me:

"Mary, I need you to tear up your list. Don't you think I know your heart better than you do? Will you trust Me?"

I chose to step into a place of full surrender. Repentant, I took the tiny mustard seed of faith in this area of life and said, "God I choose to trust You with my heart, and I choose to trust You with Peter and my relationship with him." I'm not saying lists are wrong. But in my case, my list had become an idol of what I believed was God's "perfect" man for my life. As I stepped into trust, I had faith to believe that I was hearing God. I could trust that I was clearly hearing God speak to me as He began to tell me about who Peter is in His eyes.

In 2006, Peter and I got engaged for the second time on the gorgeous northern Nungwi beaches of Zanzibar Island—off the coast of Tanzania. We were walking the beach, and suddenly (for the second time), he knelt down on one knee. This time, he was in the white sands, the music of the ocean was crashing around us, and my heart was beating fast. Instead of beating out of fear, my heart was beating from excitement. He pulled the ring out again for the second time, and I knew there was no looking back.

As the ocean waters washed around us, and with him holding steadfast on one knee, looking up at me with those baby blues, it seemed as if the world stood still and all of Heaven held its breath as he repeated those words once more: "Mary, will you marry me?" This time my heart didn't hesitate. "Yes!" I replied, and he slipped the ring on my finger for the second time.

As I stood there, tears streaming down my face, I looked up at the vastness of the Indian ocean waters as I clung to Peter. The song "How Great Is Our God" by Chris Tomlin played over and over again in my head. In that moment, I knew God had brought us full circle. *Yes, I chose you* was the cry of my heart.

As I write this, we have been happily married for almost 19 years. Has it been easy? I would say easier than some marriages.

However, like all couples, we've had our ups and downs—our share of valleys and mountain tops—and have had to fight for connection in some seasons. Going through our breakups before marriage, working out the fears in our hearts, and learning to trust gave us an easier first year of marriage. It gave us tools that we've used in our marriage and have helped many others through the years. Peter is a rock, and next to Jesus, he is *my* rock. To this day, I can say that he is everything I never knew I needed. Peter is my steady and the steady of our family. Everywhere we go, people love him because of how genuine and compassionate he is. He may not preach to the masses (although one day he just might), but he is a pastor through and through, pastoring the hearts of many in the church world and in everyday life. He has a steady love for God, for me, for our four children, for his family, and for the people around him. To know him is to love him. Through him loving our children so well and being a great father to many other spiritual children, I have learned more and more about the heart of the Father and how to lean into greater trust.

Activating our mustard seed faith to step into trust is truly a choice. I could have stayed mad or disappointed in God over all my broken relationships, but instead I chose to trust. By faith, I believed He is good and that He cared about the dreams of my heart. I chose to trust that He really did care about the promise He made to me about getting married. You know what? He was right, and He was good to His word.

I've said it before, but I will say it again: when His children ask for bread, He won't give them a stone. He is a good God. He is a good and faithful Father! As a parent, when my kids ask for something, my heart's desire is to fulfill their hearts desire. And friend, that is the heart of this loving Father over you.

Matthew 7:9–11 says:

Or what man is there among you who, when his son asks for a loaf will give him a stone? Or if he asks for a fish, he will not give him a snake, will he? If you then, being evil, know how to give good gifts to your children, how much more will your Father who is in Heaven give what is good to those who ask Him!

He is *for* you. He is for me! God is not a man that He should lie (Numbers 23:19). His word is His word. Even in our seasons of questioning or emotional weakness He doesn't abandon us. He doesn't leave us alone when we're weak and incompetent and when we feel like we can't make healthy decisions. No matter the state of our mind, heart, and emotions, in Him you have the mind of Christ, and from that place He invites us into intimacy and teaches us how to do life together with Him. Everything is an invitation into a life of greater intimacy with Him. It's a choice, and in the choosing you are powerful to partner with Him to unlock the *more* over your life and your family.

Mustard seed faith led to my "I do" as I stepped into greater faith. I took that little mustard seed of faith and chose to trust Him for my husband. I didn't know what it would look like, but all these years later, I am so grateful and in awe of God. Together with our children, God has allowed us to travel to many nations, live on two continents, pour into many people, and pour into many spiritual children. I am so grateful that God has taught me to really trust as I walked out this life of faith. Year after year, the tests come—some more than others. Yet time after time, we continue to see the goodness of God over our lives in every valley and on every mountain top. *He is that good!*

Chapter 9

The Goodness Of God

He really is that good. So good! We hear that line often as a cliché, but for me and my family, it's become more than just a line; it is our anchor of truth. We have come to a place where we know it's true no matter the situation, good or bad. We believe with all of our heart that He is good, whether or not good things happen to us. It's easy for anyone to believe He is good when life seems great, free of difficulty and disappointment. When the storms of life hit, this truly determines if we hold to this belief as an anchor in our personal lives. There were times I truly believed it, until a season of pain made me realize I didn't fully. I knew it in my mind but not fully in my heart as a core belief. Eventually, I had to come face to face with my unbelief. It would be years before I realized I finally, truly believed it at a core level. GOD IS GOOD!

Can you honestly say the phrase *God is good* is one of your core beliefs? You may have just answered *yes, 100%* in your mind, but dig deep. Ask yourself, *Is it really my core belief that God is good?* Only when you are greatly challenged and shaken in this area does the truth of your core beliefs come out.

It was August 8 of 2024, and two-days prior, we got back home from spending six weeks in Tanzania, Africa. It was the first time we'd been back there in five years after coming off the mission field fulltime and to the USA in 2019. We had seen God radically provide financially, bringing in a little over $20,000 to cover my family's six plane tickets and our on-the-ground expenses for the trip and some of our stateside expenses while we were gone. Now, here we were, back in the States after six weeks of mission life, just in time for the kids to start school. They were so excited, yet Peter and I knew the financial situation we were still in when it came to their schooling. We desperately needed to see God come through; we needed a financial miracle.

We had been praying since before we went to Africa, for God to provide the money for us to be able to pay off our kid's 2023–2024 school bill, which was $10,000 that had accumulated, since jobs had become scarce and there wasn't much work coming our way for us to make all the money we needed to pay bills, our rent, and their school fee. We also needed more just to be able to re-enroll our kids back into school for the new 2024-2025 school year, once we were all caught up on the previous bill. We thought we would have some monies owed to us come in and also have some things we were trying to sell sold by the time we got back to America to pay off the school fees in time, but unfortunately, that hadn't happened.

The first day of school was the following Tuesday, and there was no money coming in. We'd check the mailbox daily and our bank account too, but there was nothing. We felt defeated in the natural realm, and yet as a family, we kept holding onto hope. Our oldest daughter, Hope, was 16 at the time, and she turned to me that morning with tears in her eyes and loudly and passionately declared:

"Mom, we have seen God do it over and over again. He provided for us to get to Africa for six weeks...why wouldn't He do it for these school fees. He will! And we can't think any different!"

When she said this, it was a jolt, like a bolt of lightning hit me. Immediately, I felt the presence of God. It was like He was shouting, "I'VE GOT THIS!" and all I had to do was come into agreement with His *yes* and *amen* over the whole situation!

The huge financial miracle (over $20,000) for our family to get back to Africa was yet another memorial stone of remembrance in our lives.

Memorial stones can be found in several places in the Bible, but one of my favorite stories comes from Genesis 35:15. Jacob set up a stone pillar at the place where God had talked with him. He poured out a drink offering on it, and he also poured oil on it. Also, stones of remembrance are in Joshua 4:1–8. After the Israelites crossed over the Jordan, God had one man from each tribe chose a stone and set it up as a memorial for future generations to see and remember God's miraculous hand over them. Memorial stones are a reminder of the Lord's love, His kingship, His provision, and His covering over us. When we remember what He's done in the past for us and how He's provided, healed, or come through in some other way, it becomes an anchor for us and for others who hear our testimony. When we remember, it also helps us to attach our faith to the next breakthrough we need in our lives.

We held onto hope in a good God for the breakthrough. Instead of partnering with worry that day, we choose to go to the park as a family and play. Right before we left the house, we gathered as a family at home and prayed very specifically for every bit of the school monies to come in. We were excited and expectant for the miracle. No sooner had we arrived at the park when we ran into a friend who was the mother of two of our girls' friends who went to the same school as our kids. She was super excited and started sharing a testimony of how someone had paid her kids' school fees in full that week. We were excited. She had no idea of our situation and how it was so timely for us to hear her testimony! Our faith was pumped up, and we told her about our situation, asking her to pray over us for the same blessing.

Her testimony was a gateway for greater faith to rise up in us—to believe for the financial miracle. We *chose* to believe, and we were attaching faith to her testimony. *If God could do it for her and her kids, then He'll do it for us.* My daughter Naomi who was only 11 at the time prayed,

"Do it again, Lord, do it AGAIN!"

There we were, stepping into wild faith. Our family is known for our crazy faith, and I believe God likes it when we stand and believe Him for what seems like the impossible!

A couple of mornings later, my daughter Faith, who was 14 at the time, tells her sisters,

"Imagine if our truck sells today and we get that money."

Faith lives up to her name well. Later that very same day, Peter had someone out of the blue reach out to him wanting to buy our truck. We had been trying for a while to sell our big, old red truck, known as "Big Red,"—since before leaving for Africa—and suddenly it sells for $2,600. We were ecstatic, and right away we were swept up in celebrating the suddenly of God.

The next day, we paid $2,000 toward our school fees, and the other $600 from the sale was exactly what we needed for the rest of our rent money! Later that same day, we also had someone randomly send us $100. We were all so undone by the end of the day. It was like God gave us another stake and another anchor to firmly thrust into the ground to declare the truth that *God, You are good, You see us, You know everything we're walking through, and we continue to choose to trust!*

When our truck sold, we took it as a sign, celebrating that God *was* moving on our behalf! The more we have journeyed this life of faith with Jesus, we've seen over and over again how God will come through. He will do it one way or another, but usually it's different than what we expect or think. In seasons of waiting and in every season, we choose to lean in and celebrate every breakthrough, big or small.

One thing we have learned is that we don't live by this earthly economy. We choose to live by Heaven's economy!

One thing we have learned is that we don't live by this earthly economy. We choose to live by Heaven's economy! There is no lack in Heaven.

It was the day before school started, and I went school shopping with the kids in faith, buying all their class supplies. Later in the evening, we went to a sendoff for a young couple who were heading overseas to be full-time missionaries for the first time in Indonesia. As a spiritual mother and father, we knelt beside them, praying over them and asking God to provide every step of the way. In my heart as we prayed, I was declaring this over the provision of my children's school fees as well. We got home, hurrying the kids to get ready for bed, and they were buzzing about how the next day was the first day of school. Faith, right before bed, had checked her Bible app scripture for the day (which I didn't know she even had that app), and she excitedly shared the verse from James 1:2–3:

Consider it pure joy, my brothers and sisters, whenever you face trials of many kinds, because you know that the testing of your faith produces perseverance.

We knew God was speaking! I tucked my kids in bed, and my 11-year-old Naomi wanted so badly to have the assurance that she would get to go to school the next day. She is my one child who has a huge need for people and couldn't wait to be back in the school atmosphere. That night as I tucked her in, the natural realm of reality started to set in, and she started to break. She asked, "What are we going to do, Mom, if the money doesn't come by morning?"

My heart broke for her, and in that moment, I could feel the enemy of doubt trying to creep in. But the little mustard seed of faith rose up in me, and my reply was, "God has never let us down! We will keep standing in faith!" Usually, I would be a hot mess in a puddle of tears, but not this time. I could feel my faith attach to that declaration, and my heart was *instantly* at total peace.

Over the years prior to this, God had really worked on me around steadfast faith—not being wishy washy or double minded.

James 1:6–8 says,

But let him ask in faith, with no doubting, for the one who doubts is like a wave of the sea that is driven and tossed by the wind. For that person must not suppose that he will receive anything from the Lord; he is a double-minded man, unstable in all his ways.

As I was leaving her room, she was whimpering in bed, so I turned around to hold her hand. I left her that night sniffling in bed. No sooner had I walked out of her room and into mine, when there was Peter following me in. I could tell by the look on his face something good just happened. He said, “Someone just sent us $400 and another person $50!” Both of us cried with tears in our eyes.

Slowly but surely, God was crashing in. Now, we only needed another $9,450 by the next day, and we refused to have a plan B when we knew what God kept saying. “Trust Me!” I won’t lie; it was hard to tell our kids after they asked if they'd be in school, “Yes, but I'm not sure when!” Even though we were at peace (even that sounds like an oxymoron), some aspects of this journey felt frustrating because it still felt like the carrot before the cart. We still had money owed to us, and daily (multiple times a day) we were opening our bank account app to see if anything had come in. When I would see our same meager balance, I would hear, in the quietness of my heart, God say to me, “Mary, do you trust Me?” I knew this was a test.

The next morning, we woke up to several amazing gifts of financial love, and for that we were so grateful. Still $7,800 short of our school fees, we reluctantly told the kids they wouldn't be starting school that morning. Our youngest daughter was supposed to start 6th grade and our son 3rd grade. Our two oldest were starting on the following Friday, so they weren’t as sad and broken hearted.

That morning was tough. Peter was at work, and right away I gathered the kids to pray together, thanking God for the money and declaring that they *would* be in school the next day. All that morning, I kept checking my bank account, until I finally said, “Let me get online and update people with where our situation is at so they know how to pray, and we can give a praise report for what monies have come in thus far.” My Facebook post that morning was like a journal entry, which read,

> “Today, there were lots of tears and very real disappointment as we told the kids they couldn’t go to school. I held my daughter as she

wept hard and was grieving the fact that she has NEVER had to miss the first day of school. She will never get the excitement of the first day of 6th grade back, nor will my son for 3rd grade. That hurts deeply as a parent; my heart grieves with them."

In my heart of hearts, I know and hold to the fact that God is good, but it doesn't take away from the disappointment we experience. It's very real, but it's what we *do* with the disappointment that matters. It's a choice. Myself, Peter, and our children can let the disappointment shape our belief system. In doing this, we would relegate it to a lesser biblical theology of false truth; we'd come into agreement with false beliefs that God is good only sometimes, He provides for some and not for others, we did something wrong, He heals some but not others, or that healing or provision isn't for today...

Does this sound familiar?

Or, we can choose to believe perfect theology: the God of the Bible. HE is perfect theology, and it doesn't always make sense to our logical minds, but we know He is faithful. HE is our Provider and still provides. HE is our Healer and still heals. HE still cares, HE is always speaking, and HE is for us not against us! With this school situation, and maybe your own situation, it may not look exactly as what we thought in this natural realm. However, *He is a supernatural God*! HE doesn't operate in this earthly realm or this world's system as we do. He is always on time, even though in our natural state of mind we may feel like He isn't. The reality is, He *is* right on time! He is always a good Provider, He is *the* Healer, and is always the faithful One no matter the situation! When it doesn't turn out how we

> When it doesn't turn out how we thought it would, the truth is He cares about our disappointments and what we weep over.

thought it would, He cares about our disappointments and what we weep over.

Think of Mary of Bethany—Lazarus's sister. She was deeply grieved and disappointed when Lazarus died. Four days had passed, and he was in the grave. She was hurting! Jesus finally arrived to see them, and in His great love for them, He wept with her even though He *knew* the Father would still resurrect Lazarus.

I wrapped up my long Facebook post that day with:

"We know the Father will still resurrect this situation. We don't know how, we don't know when, but we know He is good, He is our Provider who *will* come through!

Although it's painful in the moment and feels like we are being squeezed, He is building perseverance and greater unshakable faith in our family that will grow a legacy! We praise God that we only need $7,800 now to get them into school this week. We still stand and still refuse to have a plan B when we know what God keeps speaking. "Trust Me!" So, we stand! We stand in spite of the frustration and the disappointment of the carrot being before the cart, knowing we have money that's owed to us, but it's not here yet. In the midst of hurt, we praise Him as a family and celebrate what He has financially given thus far, continuing to take this as a sign that GOD IS MOVING on our behalf! This situation doesn't take Him by surprise!"

I sat with my computer, spilling my heart in the Facebook journal entry/post. Once I was done, I put my computer down and noticed the house was very quiet. *Where are the kids?* I looked outside only to find them, after missing their first day of school and having a rough morning with many tears, painting and listening to worship music! My Mama heart swelled. I was so proud of them. God had settled their hearts. Their trust was in Him. They had faith!

Not much later that afternoon, I opened up my bank app on my phone one more time, and my stomach flipped. My heart skipped a beat. The money owed to us had dropped into our bank account, and God was like,

"See, I got you! The school fees are paid in full."

Unbeknownst to us, that morning at 11 a.m., the school office staff and the school board had taken time out to specifically pray for our family, bombarding Heaven for a release of finances. WON'T HE DO IT! God came through, not on our timeline, yet He came through!

You should have heard the shouts of excitement from my kids when I told them. The first thing we did was gather together, hold hands, and thank the Lord through tears.

Whatever circumstance we found ourselves in, we have always worked hard and did what we could with what God has given us. What God desires most, though, isn't a work hard slave mentality. He desires us to work smart as a son or daughter from a place of rest, knowing He's got us while we put our hands to the plow and partner with Him. Learn to trust Him, learn to let Him move however He wants to. The journey may not always feel good, yet in it, He has shown us over and over that no matter how it feels, His ways are better and higher than ours. I can promise you it's worth it, and it's all unto something bigger than you. Leaning into your mustard seed faith, walking in trust, and making a conscious choice to partner with Him opens the door to understanding your destiny; it unlocks legacy over your life.

It's so important to get vulnerable and real with God and with yourself. Do you really trust Him? In moments like we've experienced, when we didn't have the school fees, didn't know where we were going to live, or didn't know where our next meal would come from, I had to get real with myself. *Mary, do you really trust Him?*

Below, I've written out some questions that I'd highly encourage you to take time to answer. Find a quiet place, and spend some time with the Father as you ponder these questions.

Do I really trust God to handle situations that are beyond my control?

____

____

____

____

____

____

____

____

____

What areas of my life are lacking in trust?

____

____

____

____

____

____

____

____

____

What areas of my life do I need to surrender to God?

How can I better align my heart with the truths of God's Word over my life and the situations I find myself in?

Chapter 10

Legacy

Getting real and honest with ourselves, our hearts, and with God is life changing because in that place of leaning in, wholeness can come. When we are healthy, things come into alignment and we begin to live for the future, not just today. Our desire to make Christ known leads us to build toward leaving a lasting legacy.

At this stage of my life, legacy is something I am extremely passionate about. Leaving a legacy happens when we choose to grow and to step into what we were created for. I grew up understanding family origins but never had a grid for legacy, much less the importance of building a family legacy.

Honestly, I didn't even know what legacy really meant. The word "legacy" itself can have several meanings depending on the context it's used in, but at its core, it refers to something that's left behind or inherited from the past. When people think of legacy, they typically talk about things like property, money, or a responsibility that's handed down from one generation to the next.

For example, someone might inherit a family business, a house, or a sum of money as part of their family legacy, or they could inherit a trait, like being a welder or a writer. And while these are all good things, they're a type of "passed down" legacy in the natural, physical form. But there is also Kingdom legacy. When it comes to the "Kingdom legacy" I'm referring to, it's a spiritual legacy that grows much wider and deeper as it expands into the generations after you. What I have grown to realize is Kingdom legacy creates impact and leaves a contribution, not only in society, but also in your sphere of Kingdom influence. It touches your family, your children, your children's children, your spiritual children, a movement, a city, a country, and even the nations.

My day-to-day life growing up was focused on survival without thinking about the future much. There was no thought of building for the future of my children, my future grandchildren, or my great-grandchildren, their children, spiritual sons and daughters, or anyone else. I had no understanding that my family legacy could greatly impact the spiritual realm just by raising up spiritual children who would create wakes of legacy with their own footprints on the world stage.

I am now living proof of how mustard seed faith can grow a tree that has a family legacy. This tree can have an impact into your direct family line and as I've seen, even into the nations. When it comes to legacy, I was the least likely candidate to be a person of great faith. Now, I have a husband and kids who love Jesus, but it wasn't always like that, as you've gathered from the glimpses I've shared throughout this book. I had all the odds stacked against me. I was the least likely person to be leaving a great family legacy to my children, their children, and my spiritual children here in the USA and in the nations of the world.

The words I've penned in this book—a window into my past—don't do justice to the raw truth. If I could give you the up close and personal, full-on view into my past experiences, with all the pain, hurts, abuse, trauma, neglect, negative hurtful words spoken over me and about me, negative self-talk, the suicidal thoughts, and more, you would never think I would have a good legacy to pass down. But my legacy has transformed to being a Jesus lover, a college graduate, a missionary, a teacher, a preacher, a transformational life coach, a business owner several times over, an author, a podcaster, a wife, and a mother with huge dreams. In some ways, as I write this book, I feel like I'm just getting started.

A huge part of the success I have achieved in life is because of the countless people God has sent across my path over the years. Having lots of people impact my life was great, but there were two pivotal women who directly contributed to why I'm alive today and why I am who I am. I owe a lot to the prayers of my late Grandmother Mitsu Horiuchi Stokley (known as Bachan to many of her grandkids and great-grands), and as I mentioned in previous chapters, my amazing spiritual mom and sister-like friend Beth.

My Grandmother Mitsu chose to partner with and step into her mustard seed faith and pray into me when I was just a baby, throughout my adolescent, teen, and adult years, and especially when I went to the mission field. My grandmother wasn't perfect, but she did her best. She was a meek and quiet woman—the daughter of Japanese Shintoist immigrants who came to America hoping for a better life. She was taught to be seen and not heard as a submissive Japanese girl, and she carried that into her adult life.

During her college years, she got saved, and she had dreams to become a horticulturalist. She was gentle in spirit, so much so, she could get a bee to land on her finger and she would pet it. I have fond memories of her watering her many plants and even singing to them. She could make any plant come to life. She was an incredible wood carver and would make ornate, beautiful Victorian-like doll houses and little furniture to go with it and weaved floor rugs. She was also an incredible seamstress, making wedding dresses for people and more. She was just someone who really could excel at anything she put her hands to. She carried her meekness into her marriage, but when she got into her prayer closet, she was bold and believed God at His Word.

In front of us grandkids, she was a praying woman and represented God well. I can remember seeing her often praying with her Bible open, even into her last years when I would visit her in Colorado. When I was a child, I can remember standing next to her in her Baptist Church and singing songs out of the hymnal. I loved hearing her sing, and I would look up at her, and it was as if her face glowed with the love of Jesus. She would also pull out her harpsicord or her mandolin and sing for us grandkids when we visited her at her little apartment.

She didn't really preach to us much, but she lived and spoke the truths of the Word of God over us. She corrected us in love and led us, not so much with her words but more by her actions of great faith. In our eyes, she was extremely gifted in many ways and a saint who could do no wrong. As an adult looking back, I can see her flaws. In the midst of them, to us, she was our perfect grandma who had a love for God that was tangible to all who met her. People were drawn to her warmth and her deep love. We all were drawn to her warm smile, her inviting amazing hugs, and her wisdom. She often adopted many people as her "kids."

In May of 2022, my grandmother joined the cloud of witnesses. I know she's looking down from Heaven and cheering us on—cheering on our dreams to build a greater family legacy. To say I miss her is an understatement. I owe a lot to her dedication and her prayers.

Prayers are never to be underestimated. I believe it was the prayers of my grandmother and my Beth that kept me alive and helped shape me to be the God- fearing woman I am today. When I was 12 years old, Beth came into my life. It was in a season of my life when I was in a broken, single-parent home. My mother wasn't always around much, but she did take us to church, and for that I'm forever grateful.

Prayers are never to be underestimated.

At our church when I was 12, I was allowed to join the youth group. Beth and her husband Bill served under our youth pastor as youth leaders, and it was there where I met them. Beth saw me. I believe the Lord allowed her to see me with her spiritual eyes, and that's why she pursued my heart. I never spoke to people much, staying quiet and withdrawn. As you can imagine from my previous chapters, I had major trust issues.

Youth group was a place of escape for me—from my troubles and the emotional conflicts of my home life. I usually was able to go to youth group on Wednesday nights, although at times it was conditional. I could only go if I had a ride there and had a ride home. Beth began to take me home every Wednesday night. I was drawn to her right away. She was 27 at the time—beautiful, young, vivacious, funny, and I really looked up to her. Internally, I wondered why she wanted to even have me around because I never felt pretty enough, smart enough, or good enough to measure up to her. I loved her right away, but I couldn't understand her love and kindness toward me. Even so, as a young girl with an orphaned heart, I hungered for it and was drawn to it.

Every week for an entire year, she would fill the car with her friendly voice and funny stories while I listened, but I hardly said a peep. We laugh about it now, but she often would ask the Lord something along the lines of, *Oh my goodness, God, how much longer do I have to do this? Is she ever gonna talk?* Little did she know, those rides home were activating my mustard seed of faith which eventually helped me to trust, and that led me to open up to her, telling her all about my upbringing in physical abuse, sexual abuse, bad neglectful home life, and more.

At some point she had given me her number, and I would sneak the phone and call her, asking what she was doing, hoping she would ask me if I wanted to come over on the weekend or sometimes before youth. Eventually, it just became a thing. She brought me into her home on the weekends, and those weekends turned into years of relationship with a healthy family—spending time with people who had hearts full of Jesus and His love.

I adored her and held her in such high esteem. I walked through both her pregnancies with her and loved helping her with her house and the kids every week. I loved her kids so deeply as if they were my own. God allowed me to be in her life so I could learn how to be a loving wife and good, loving mother. We may not get to see each other as often or talk as much as we used to, but I fiercely love them even to this day. My heart is so full because of her. My children and my spiritual children have benefitted because of her. I owe so much of who I am today to Beth and Bill.

When I married Peter, I'll never forget Beth telling me what one of the ministers (Pastor Reddock) said to her after Peter and I had one of our pre-marital counseling sessions with him. He said, "Beth, now I know why she is marrying Peter. He's just like Bill." I picked an amazing man, and I am the wife I am today to my husband because of the amazing woman Beth was to me growing up.

Both of these women and their relationships with God planted and grew in me a mustard seed faith of spiritual and tangible family legacy. Everything I've done, everything I do, and everything I have yet to become, I believe, will be part of their reward in Heaven.

Creating family legacy is fully stepping into and activating that mustard seed of faith, knowing it's a faith shaped by stepping into trust in Jesus. Through this trust, we make choices and create core values that make up who we are and what we pass on to future generations. When choosing to step into this little seed form of faith, the choices we make in our lives with conviction, guided by a trust and greater faith in God, can and will lead to a life that's tangibly marked by legacy—in you and your family. People will see you are a person marked by honor, truth, integrity, passion, compassion, and servitude. They will see your legacy unlocked as you lean in and choose to trust your journey with the Father. They will see how well you love by seeing how you serve people as Jesus did—at the highest levels. This is what grows a family legacy. Jesus created a legacy of servitude by washing His disciples' feet, even the very one He knew would betray Him for 30 pieces of silver.

This faith and love in God can serve as a thread that connects different generations within a family line, both in the natural and the in the spiritual. Parents just like me who've taken mustard seed faith and stepped into trust while walking through the valleys have come out stronger on the other side. We've taken our scars and laid them at the feet of Jesus, choosing to let Him heal our past, choosing to let Him into every area of our heart. By doing this, we've been able to rise up with our badges of authority and honor, while passing on our faith to our children, creating a sense of identity and shared purpose. I believe this *will* extend through the generations of our family line and into the generations of our spiritual children.

I love this verse in Joshua 24:15:

As for me and my house we will serve the Lord.

This verse shouts "family legacy" from the rooftops. I've fought hard through the valleys of fear, brokenness, not good enough, never going to amount to much, shame, and dashed dreams that felt so unattainable and ones I thought people would laugh at, but yet here I am. I am a walking billboard for mustard seed faith that has helped me trust in this beautiful Jesus, find my roar, and build for legacy. When others witness the transformation and impact mustard seed faith has on someone's life like mine, it usually inspires them to also believe that it *is* possible to unlock it in their own lives and to step into trust over their own futures.

My goal is to inspire people around the world to trust God, and fall in love with this wonderful Savior. I want them to know it's possible to take that trust and allow it to catapult you into greater faith—more than you've ever known. As you take steps into the small beginnings of greater faith, you will feel the power of freedom it brings you. It creates momentum, creates change, and builds legacy in your own life.

I hope you're getting the picture I'm trying to paint. Legacy is what you carry inside you to create and build when you step out and unlock mustard seed faith, and it's how you allow the Kingdom of Heaven to shine through you to leave an impact here on earth. Legacy is what flows out of us when we choose to take the tools we gain by going through things in life and the gifts God created us with and let them ignite a greater faith to use them powerfully. When we steward our core values, our gifts, and our talents, legacy is released and imparted to influence the beliefs, values, and behaviors of future generations. The lessons we've learned from the past can shape current and future decisions and change our family's trajectory.

Have you ever thought about the fact that what you choose to do today can make or break future generations in your family line? That's a hefty thought, isn't it. It's true! The actions and choices influenced by mustard seed faith in our lives today can leave a lasting impact on the world. God is love, so letting love lead, creating acts of kindness, showing generosity and selflessness, and having a servant's heart, driven by a little tiny mustard seed of faith, can create *huge* change. The change continues to flow like a river into generations you may never get to lay eyes on. Your mustard seed faith can unlock legacy that literally influences the beliefs, values, and behaviors of future generations and could quite possibly even help shift a whole culture. This blows my mind to think like this! Sometimes when I think this deep, the responsibility of my actions and words feel daunting and yet so exciting.

We are not here on earth to merely exist; we are here because each one of us is born with a purpose. You are reading this book, still a live, still living and breathing. Guess what? *You are born for a purpose*! Yes, *you*! Some are born to leave a mark on a global scale, while others are born to impact and touch the lives of those in your circle of influence in powerful, meaningful ways. Finding purpose in life starts with mustard seed faith, and creating a lasting legacy is a profound journey that requires your mustard seed of faith. It takes faith to step into your *yes* to Jesus. Faith requires you to take risks, take action, and navigate your way through the valleys and the mountain tops of life, letting Jesus lead.

The quest for true legacy begins with finding your purpose. What makes you come alive? What brings you joy? What gifts and talents do you possess that you know God has given you? Unlocking legacy requires a deep dive into the heart of God, creating a value system of Heaven over your passions and your strengths. It's understanding what makes you cry and what makes you laugh as you open your heart to Jesus. By taking the time to give God your heart and to understand how He created you, you'll discover what truly resonates with you and what gives your life meaning. Leaning into His heart of love is a crucial starting point; it activates your mustard seed faith and helps you to step into truth, and from there, you can walk in greater faith and create lasting legacy. Through this self-discovery with Jesus, you can unearth the passions that lead you to your purpose, allowing them to serve as a compass for releasing legacy in your life, both in the spiritual realm and in the natural.

The actions and choices influenced by mustard seed faith in our lives can leave a lasting impact on the world.

Knowing *whose* you are, who you are, and knowing your purpose creates opportunities for you to take tangible action steps to build a lasting legacy. Building legacy isn't about your money, and it isn't about seeking fame or recognition in your school, your church, your business, your job, your music, or even in the book you're writing. It's about making Jesus known and leaving a meaningful mark on the world—one that outlives you and causes Jesus to shine through it all. It involves setting goals and aligning your daily choices with your purpose, whether that's through your career, relationships or community involvement, etc. Settling for nothing less than integrity and excellence in everything you do, while serving people at the highest level, all helps to build legacy.

When you read through the Gospels, you find that Jesus was the greatest servant of all. He left behind a blueprint for you and me in how to build an incredible legacy. His legacy still impacts the world today. Now, I know some of you reading this will think, *Yes! But that was Jesus! I'm not like Him.* Nobody is asking you to *be* Jesus, but we are made in His image and we can grow to be *like* Him. Being Christlike means possessing His heart for mankind. You will never be Jesus! I'm merely saying to be yourself, knowing and fully grasping the truth that you were created in the image of God. You carry His DNA, and He lives in *you*.

The Bible tells us in John 14:12 that all we have to do is *believe*. Stepping into your mustard seed faith will also carry you into this greater realm of belief, helping you believe that *you will do greater works than Him*! He believes in you, and I believe in you!

Do you believe in you?

He loves you, friend, and He is shouting His approval of "Yes!" and "Amen!" over you. Will you believe Him and take Him at His Word? The Bible declares His promises over you; His Word is *powerful*, and His promises are YES and AMEN!

John 14:12 says,

Truly, truly, I say to you, he who believes in Me, the works that I do, he will do also; and greater works than these he will do; because I go to the Father.

This kind of belief in Jesus comes from growing deep faith roots. Have you found that little seed of faith? Growing and cultivating a little mustard seed of faith is truly like nurturing a delicate sapling in the garden of your heart and mind. At first, it can seem insignificant. There's nothing really to look at and hardly anything to tend to...until there is. A regular seed in a garden can seem barely noticeable until it begins to sprout.

Several summers ago, I wanted to try my hand at gardening. I knew that as I placed seed in the ground, it would exercise and grow the seed of faith inside me to believe it would sprout. Each week, I worked to pull out the weeds so they didn't choke out the seeds. My seeds eventually sprouted, and I grew corn, zucchini, cucumbers, bell peppers, and more.

> Growing and cultivating a little seed of faith is truly like nurturing a delicate sapling in the garden of your heart and mind.

Mustard seed faith can seem barely noticeable among the weeds of doubts and uncertainties. When doubts, uncertainties, and bad beliefs come along and bombard your mind, it's time to tend to your garden of faith and walk into trust. Stand on the truth that God is for you and that He loves you and wants the best for you. With patience, care, and standing on unwavering belief, the tiny seed of faith can flourish into a mighty tree with deep roots of trust. That very tree will start to release hope, offering shade and shelter to your soul, while you continuously prune it and take care of it to build for great legacy.

Just as a tree requires nourishment, sunlight, and protection, faith also demands constant attention. We have to be willing to take our mustard seed of faith, step out, and speak truth. Why? Because the power of life and death are in our tongue (Proverbs 18:21). We have to renew our minds with the Word of God, with hope, with truth, and expose it to the sunlight of our Heavenly Father's Kingdom realm. We have to shield our mind from the storms of doubt, skepticism, and self-sabotage. When we do, watch as faith takes root, grows, and thrives. In the end, a once-small seed transforms into an unshakeable foundation, unlocking trust, causing you to step into hope and thrive while you build for legacy.

You were created for more! Don't let the lies of your past, your present, or the world tell you any different. You are the head and not the tail (Deuteronomy 28:13). You have one life to live, so make it count. Let your tree grow deep, far, and wide, and live your life to the fullest, allowing yourself to step into who Love says you are. *Remember, God is Love*! In Him your sure foundation is found. In Him you will be like a deeply rooted tree, planted by the rivers of water, always green, always full of life, spreading your branches far and wide, never failing to bear much fruit.

It's time to trust. It's time to hope again. It's time to allow your faith to grow a tree of legacy as His promises over you become more evident day by day. Can you hear Him? He is shouting His *yes* and *amen* over you, friend, and over your life! It's time! Who is waiting on you to release your faith and grow a tree of legacy?

Take some time to quiet yourself before the Lord and ask Him some questions. It's time to dream with God. Friend, I believe He gets excited when you choose to partner with Him and dream with Him. Allow the very things you carry—your gifts, your talents, and your heart for mankind—to come forth as you co-create with Him, building His Kingdom together on earth as it is in Heaven. He's waiting to release His *yes and amen* over you and the legacy of your life.

Sit with the Lord and ponder these questions:

What are the dreams in my heart, and what does legacy look like for me?

Who am I called to impact?

(Write it out as God stirs your heart. For me, I have to capture it in the moment or voice record it on my phone so I don't forget.)

Chapter 11

His Promises Are Yes And Amen

Looking back over my life, through the abuse, the trauma, my broken family, the lingering orphan mindset, relationship betrayals, relationship breakups, the poverty and poverty mindset, and the near-death experiences, I can honestly say that God has never left me powerless or desolate. He will never leave *you* powerless or desolate either. You may *feel* that way, but the reality is, His promises over us are *yes* and *amen*. As I've woven bits and pieces of my experiences and life stories throughout this book, my hope is that it has encouraged you, brought healing, brought freedom, and is unlocking your faith and greater trust in our good, good Father. If God can do it for me, He can do it for you. My life is living proof that this is true.

Second Corinthians 1:20 says,

For as many as are the promises of God, in Him they are yes; therefore, also through Him is our Amen to the glory of God through us.

His Word is full of promises over us and promises that are for us. When His Word goes forth, He tells us it will not return void or empty without accomplishing what He desires.

Isaiah 55:11 says,

So will My word be which goes forth from My mouth; it will not return to Me empty, without accomplishing what I desire, and without succeeding in the matter for which I sent it."

God's Word is far from empty. Let me say that again; let it sink into your heart...*God's Word is far from empty*! There is power in His Word. His Word also holds an abundance of promises, and guess what? He truly desires to fulfill each and every promise in us, over us, and through us.

God's promises over us are a firm declaration of truth. When God makes a promise, He makes an unbreakable commitment to fulfill it. The "Yes" in His promises over us are louder than what our yes to Him will ever be. He is 100% for us and not against us. I can just hear Him shouting over you right now, "Yes, My daughter!" or "Yes, My son!" And it's so simple to receive the fullness of His promises. Simply choose to trust, and you will see by faith that He is for you. His very nature is good, His faith lives in us, and the Word of God is active through us. That little seed of faith inside you will create momentum in your life.

As you step into the mustard seed faith and seek Him with your whole heart, you *will* find Him (Jeremiah 29:13). You will know His voice over you. You will know Him and you will hear Him. I am convinced that stepping into your small, little mustard seed of faith has the power to bring you into the divine knowledge of His presence—which is daily living and abiding in you. Every single day you wake up and give Him your *yes*, the mustard seed of faith is taking you from strength to strength, glory to glory, building you and making you stronger. It will bring you into an understanding of His divine nature, of His divine plan for your life, and of His divine holiness in and through you.

I hope you have seen throughout this book how faith is always active; it never lies dormant. It will only grow when we choose to take hold of it and allow it to grow. Faith is the hand of God and the power of God living in and through our lives. Faith is never double minded, it never fears, and it doesn't waiver. Faith simply doesn't doubt!

Faith is the hand of God and the power of God living in and through our lives.

Faith stands like a tree with deep roots, unshakable, spreading it's branches far and wide, building for legacy, even in the midst of great conflict. Faith remains steadfast, even in the midst of a world that feels chaotically out of control at times. Faith moves seemingly immovable things, both in the natural realm and the spiritual realm. By faith, sin, lies, wrong beliefs, and wrong agendas are dethroned as you choose to trust in the truth of God. By faith, family lines are restored; prodigal sons and daughters are brought home and are reunited in the natural realm and with God in their hearts. By faith, wisdom and knowledge are released and received, strongholds are brought down, cities and nations are changed, business ideas are released and received, businesses are built, people are healed, demons are cast out, wealth is acquired, homes are bought, families are made, families are healed, families are brought together, and people are restored. By faith, legacy is ignited and grown, creating wakes of history around the world. By faith, revival is ignited, and throughout history, whole cities and nations have turned to Jesus.

When you step into that mustard seed faith and become a faith-filled man or woman, others will be drawn to you. People around the world, those desperate and hopeless, look to you because you have a faith that hopes when all hope seems lost.

Just the other day, I was having a conversation with someone, and the idea came up that this world seems to be getting darker and darker. When you look at circumstances with natural eyes, yes, this would seem to be true. However, what is Heaven's reality? This conversation made me smile, but not because I thought I had better *end-time theology*. The truth of the matter is, none of us know for sure what the "end" will look like. Only God has perfect theology, not man, so it's not worth arguing over. I was smiling and excited in this conversation because of Heaven's reality: the darker this world gets, the more Jesus' light will illuminate in it as His bride arises and begins to shine His light all around.

Imagine being in a dark room and a light is suddenly switched on. As the light enters the dark space, it can feel blinding at first; it's so bright and illuminates everything. You know what I'm talking about! Maybe your husband, your wife, your kids, your brother, or your sister, comes into the room after you've been in bed for a while, and you're almost asleep and they flip on the light. It feels blinding and shocking—so much so that you have to shield your eyes and blink to adjust to the light.

God's light is being flipped on, and it's beginning to illuminate every dark crevasse of this world. By faith, I believe the church—His bride—is coming out of her slumber and blinking because the light is being switched on. The church is adjusting her sight as she's arising. His light is revealing things hidden in the dark for too long, and it's blinding the eyes of the enemy.

By faith, no matter what's going on in our world, we get to step into His promises and get to step into hope against all hope because

He *is* the God of all hope; we can grab hold of the sureness of this truth by faith.

The dark crevices of my heart were illuminated with God's light over 38 years ago when I received the purple Walkman for Christmas with the simple label *"from Jesus."* This act of love activated the mustard seed faith in me.

Over the years, that little seed in my life has grown into a huge, strong tree with deep roots and branches spreading far and wide. My tree branches of faith and legacy have become supports for others and have activated faith in people. This includes activating my own children to believe for financial breakthrough in our family and to have crazy dreams that may seem impossible. Faith has been activated in many of my spiritual children too, inspiring them to dream bigger and even write books. It has helped activate my mother to believe God really does love her, she is forgiven, and He has a plan for her life. I know more healing came to her because I opened myself up to greater faith by choosing to forgive her, and it set her faith in motion to believe for heart restoration with her children. God is a restorer!

> God's light is being flipped on, and it's beginning to illuminate every dark crevasse of this world.

By faith, the enemy won't steal my family, our businesses, our finances, our joy, or our health anymore. I have learned the authority that I have in the Lord Jesus Christ. Between my husband and I, our deep-rooted, strong tree of faith has spread its branches to my children. Even though they are young, it is teaching them to dream big, to never give up, and to think and build for legacy from a young age. My tree has spread its branches here in the USA and in other nations to my spiritual children and has helped many of them walk into freedom and harness dreams in their hearts. Why do I tell you this? Because I want you to feel it, see it for yourself, and grab hold of the fact that if I can unlock my mustard seed of faith after going through what I went through in life and get the breakthrough to build a strong tree of faith of legacy, so can you.

Now that I'm nearing my 50th birthday, by faith, I am just getting started with the second half of my life. Not long ago, someone asked me the question, "If you were to die today and look back on your life, what regrets would you have because of dreams you never stepped into or things you haven't accomplished yet?" I was able to answer their question rather quickly. Looking back, I have no regrets. There have been many victories I've fought for in my life and won. Are there still things I'd like to do and accomplish? Yes. However, by God's grace I have accomplished a lot. People are astonished when they hear about my backstory and journey, and I can only give credit to the Lord Jesus Christ for rescuing and saving me. He helped me to understand that faith is simple, starting as small as a mustard seed, and that I only have to come to Him like a child. He is my Papa, and I am His daughter.

As I've leaned into the more of Him, I've noticed my dreams have only gotten bigger. I know there is more! By faith, I am stepping into the more, and my tree of faith is growing taller, wider, and bigger—the branches spreading further, wider, and greater than I could have *ever* imagined.

As your roots grow deeper and your tree grows sturdier, so does your confidence in the promises of God and the truth that with Him, *all* things are possible. As your tree grows taller and taller, you can see past the valleys, further into the dreams God has placed in your heart, and the Kingdom solutions we have access to. From that higher place comes one of the most fun opportunities: co-creating with Him. We don't *have to*...we *get to*! Can someone please give a shout!

I can feel the fire of God on me and His excitement in this statement. Ladies and gentlemen, let this sink in: we *get to* co-create with Him as His sons and daughters. Yes, I am shouting that over you right now and over myself. *WE GET TO*! He's a good Father, a wonderful Dad, and He can't wait for us to step into our faith and say *yes* to Him and the blueprints from Heaven over our lives.

Have you stepped into your mustard seed faith?

Has your root system begun to grow?

If you answered *no*, then I want to challenge you to step out. You are not behind or late! The truth is, you are right on time. Simply give your whole *yes* and you can start today!

If you answered *yes*, then well done! I'm championing you on, and I want to ask you a few more questions.

How deep are you willing to allow your roots to go, and will you allow your tree of faith to grow deep, tall, and wide?

If you are in a growth season, are you fully yielding to Him?

In reality, it takes yielding to God and partnering with Him. Yielding means to be totally surrendered and committed. It means we acknowledge that God is our Friend, our Lover, our Father, our King, our Judge, and our Savior. Yielding to Him, means praising Him in the midst of life's uncertainty and no matter what, staying grounded in the daily *yes* of yielding and declaring this:

"Jesus, Yours is the Kingdom, Yours is the power, and YOURS is the glory, forever and ever amen."

This journey is all about Him. It's not about me, and it's not about you. It is about making Him known on the earth, releasing His Kingdom on earth as it is in Heaven. It's about growing our tree of faith while yielding to Him, taking His hand and stepping into the *yes* and *amen* over your life.

What do you want your *yes* and *amen* to look like? I know I want mine to look like a huge tree of faith, one that makes people in awe of God as they look at my life—not to bring me honor, but to bring Him honor and make Him known. I want my tree to be one that brings people into the awe of God as they find peace and find rest in its branches. I want mine to continuously bring hope and life to people. I want it to create family legacy for my children, my children's children, their children, and beyond. I want it to look like legacy for my spiritual children, even bigger than what it is now, so they can go further and wider than I do. I want my yes to be so full of faith that it looks like having a huge impact around the world, releasing hope over people everywhere I speak, through international projects like our girls home in Africa, through courses we create, and the resources we release (like this book) that I believe will draw people into the Kingdom of God.

I like to call myself a prophetic strategist and a hope solutionist—even my Instagram name is *mamahope2nations*! It makes me laugh, because hope has been a lifelong theme. It makes me wonder, could our hope and faith catapult us into a *bigger yes*? It's so important for your tree of faith to create such a big *yes* that it can only be accomplished *with* Him. In Him, hope stays alive, you keep dreaming, you keep finding solutions to problems, and you keep moving forward and building God's Kingdom. May your tree of faith and your faith-filled *yes* be so big that you live like Jesus is coming back tomorrow, but you also keep dreaming and building like He isn't coming back for hundreds more years. That, my friend, is building for legacy.

When you attach your mustard seed faith to your *yes*, it becomes transformative, crossing cultural divides and international borders. It becomes like a skeleton key of authority given to you in the realm of the Spirit. Do you know what a skeleton key is? It's a key that can unlock any door. It gives you *all* access. When you are rooted in Him in *true* sonship and you step into trust, attaching your *yes* to your faith, God entrusts you with a skeleton key of Heaven. He says, "Here...now you have all access!" So, what do you want to do? What do you want to create? What do you want to build? All we have to do is ask.

When you attach your mustard seed faith to your *yes*, it becomes transformative, crossing cultural divides and international borders.

John 14:13–14 says,

> *Whatever you ask in My name, that will I do, so that the Father may be glorified in the Son. If you ask Me anything in My name, I will do it.*

Oh that Jesus would be glorified in the nations and in all we say and do! I can't help but by faith say, "Amen," and come into agreement with His *yes* and *amen* over my life. I hope and pray you do the same.

Some of you reading this book can understand and relate to the stories I've shared and the difficult circumstances I've walked through. Some of the valleys I went through felt so dark that it was hard to breathe, and I didn't know if I could get out. Yet I did, and I have come out stronger. In the midst of the valleys and hard journeys, I endured so much, but I experienced victory on the other side. Seeing so much of God coming through in unprecedented ways has birthed BIG faith within me. There is no doubt in my mind; I *know* God can move mountains through your mustard seed of faith too. Only believe!

My heart's cry is that this book encourages you to take the journey from mustard seed faith into trust in our big God so a *huge* tree of faith grows in your own life. May the branches expand into generations and generations to come, creating wakes of legacy and hope as you co-create with God. The seed is in you, and He is for you! Are you ready to jump in? I know He is ready and waiting with open arms, and His hands are extended to receive you.

Who is waiting for you to step into your mustard seed of faith and unlock your greater yes over your life's legacy?

I believe there is something you could never have imagined on the other side of your *yes*. In this moment, as you come to the end of this book, picture Jesus holding your hand. Let's take the plunge with Him and not look back; I sincerely believe it's going to be worth it all.

Friend, you have made it to the end of this book, and that tells me your heart's desire is for more. I believe your heart desires to step into greater levels of trust with God, and it desires to step into greater faith and growth. Friend, as you yield and give Him your *yes* and choose to trust, your mustard seed of faith is already growing roots. It is a daily choice, choosing to step out and trust Him one day at a time. Let's do it together!

Before you go, I invite you to declare a prayer of faith over your life. Read the prayer on the next page out loud with your mustard seed faith, and watch what God begins to do! Enjoy the journey. It's time!

Prayer Into Great Faith

Father God,

I choose to believe! With my mustard seed of faith, I choose to trust You. I recognize that faith is not just a word, it's an action.

By faith, I choose to trust You to give me the wisdom to understand how to rise above doubt, while running at all of the lies and all of the Goliaths in my path.

Thank you that as my roots of faith grow stronger, all uncertainty goes, in Jesus' name.

Thank you that as I stay grounded in You,

I have the strength to grow my faith to be as resilient as a mustard tree, bending and swaying with the winds of change, yet strong, wide, and firmly rooted in You to build for legacy.

Thank you for the strength to overcome in moments of weakness and fear, knowing that as I choose You and stand in my faith, I will be able to overcome any valley of life's storms.

I thank you that as I step into faith I will receive all that You say I am and all that You have for me.

Father, thank you for the grace to see the beauty that exists, even during trials, and to trust that every experience, both past and present, is an opportunity for greater growth and an invitation into closer intimacy with You.

Thank you that You are growing BIG faith within me that unlocks trust, hope, and patience and grows the mind of Christ in me as You rewire my belief system to think from Your Kingdom perspective.

Thank you for Your unwavering heart and Your steadfast love for me, and how You will grow me and teach me in all Your ways.

I declare that my faith will be a sturdy tree of truth, hope, and love and that it will be a beacon of trust and truth in the darkness.

Jesus, thank you for my faith that will continue to flower, blossom, and shine, creating a path for others to follow because of my life lived in alignment with You and for Your divine purpose.

Thank you for a faith to grow a tree that will impact people and grow a legacy. In Jesus' name! I choose You!

Amen.

Jeremiah 17: 7–8 says,

Blessed is the man who trusts in the LORD, and whose trust is the LORD. For he will be like a tree planted by the water, that extends its roots by a stream; and will not fear when the heat comes; But its leaves will be green; And it will not be anxious in a year of drought, nor cease to yield fruit.

IT DOESN'T HAVE TO BE COMPLICATED

As you have journeyed through this book with me, maybe you find yourself reading and questioning, *Do I even really know God?* Maybe you've had bad "Christian" role models in your life, and this "Christianity" thing has felt more like it's full of hyper faith, hypocrites, or fakeness instead of truth, love, joy, or peace. Maybe you have just fallen away from God, and through hurts, disappointments, and pain, you have grown weary, finding your relationship is not what it used to be.

If you made it to the back of the book and you're reading this, it's not by accident. God knows you, and He knew you would be here, right now, in this very moment of time, with those thoughts running through your head and heart. *He knows you!* He knows you better than you know yourself. In Jeremiah 1:5, it talks about how He created you and knew you before you were even formed in your mother's womb.

He wants to be in relationship with you. He wants your heart, and His desire is that you are whole and that you choose to receive Him (or return back to Him).

I want to extend an invitation to you to discover the real Jesus—not a scary Jesus or religious Jesus, but the *real* Jesus. He is the Savior who takes our small steps of faith and turns them into something extraordinary. In Him, you will find how to truly trust and experience the forgiveness that you may long for. If your heart has drifted away from Him, you can rediscover your first love in the simple faith of trust. You will learn that it really is simple and only requires childlikeness and mustard seed faith. Taking little steps of faith forward, you will grow into *big* faith—faith, to forgive as He forgives and to build a legacy rooted in His eternal love and purpose for your life.

Friend, let me tell you...it's not about perfection, it's about stepping into a relationship with the One who loves you unconditionally! He's the One who desires to walk with you through every season of life, and by allowing Him into every area of your heart, He can transform your mustard seed of faith into something that can move mountains. The beauty of this is, He truly meets us where we're at with open arms and with never-ending love. His desire is that we come home to Him, and He is extending the invitation to you to become part of His family right now, in this very moment, and all you have to do is believe. It's that simple!

John 1:12 says,

But as many as received Him, to them He gave the right to become children of God, even to those who believe in His name...

You only have to believe in Him. Believe that He is the Son of God, that He died and rose again for you, and that He loves you because He loves you! He loves you so much He was willing to die for you so you could have eternal life with Him forever.

John 3:16 says,

For God so loved the world, that He gave His only begotten Son, that whoever believes in Him shall not perish, but have eternal life.

Do you want that?

THE INVITATION

Do you want a real love relationship with Him?

If you said *yes*, then you're already stepping into belief, and now all you have to do is confess with your mouth that Jesus is Lord. Ask Him to forgive your sins, wash you clean, and believe in your heart that Jesus is the Son of God.

Romans 10:9 says,

...that if you confess with your mouth Jesus as Lord, and believe in your heart that God raised Him from the dead; you will be saved.

When you say *yes* to a relationship with Jesus, just know there is no magical way to do this. All it takes is simply praying and asking Him to come into your heart. I want to invite you to do that with me right now. Just pray the following prayer out loud, confess with your mouth, and watch and see how He will flood your heart with His love. I believe you will feel the shift as He comes into your heart.

Jesus,

I ask that You come into my heart. I repent of my sins. I surrender my life to You.

I ask You to wash me clean from all impurities in my mind and heart.

I believe that You are Jesus Christ, the Son of God, and that You died on the cross for the forgiveness of my sins and rose again on the third day so I can live victorious in You and in right relationship with You for the rest of my life.

I confess with my mouth today and believe in my heart that You, Jesus, are my Savior and Lord from this day forward.

I choose to be in a relationship with You. I denounce religion, and I choose to grow in right relationship and love with You.

Amen!

If you prayed that prayer with me, congratulations! Welcome to the family of God! I'm so proud of you for stepping out and choosing to trust by taking a step of mustard seed faith. As you have read in this book, you know my journey wasn't easy. But, friend, let me tell you, I can truly say it has been so worth it. I've never known a love like His. He loves you more than you can ever know or imagine. As I have grown more and more in a love relationship with Him, I have discovered that He is for me, not against me. The life, love, and freedom I found in Him by stepping out in my very own mustard seed of faith is far better than I could have ever guessed. He loves us just because He loves us, and there's nothing you can do to add or take away from His love. It's who He is; He's just *that good.*

If you prayed that prayer, I highly encourage you to email us at roaringhope@gmail.com and tell a close friend who you know loves Jesus too. One of the most important things now is to get your hands on a Bible—God's written Word—and also pray and seek a Bible-believing Christian church in your area to learn more about Jesus and meet other believers who can disciple and help you on your journey. If you're not sure how to find a good church, email us and we'll help direct you the best we can.

I believe in you, and I'm excited for you to walk out your new faith, discover more of the love of Jesus, and grow more and more in love with Him.

Acknowledgements

To My Peter,

Thank you for loving me and championing me so well through every page of writing this book, Hon. You have made me think deeply, gave great honest feedback (even though I may not of always liked it), watched the kids while I hid away writing in my office (i.e., coffee shops...LOL) too many times to count, and cheered me on until I finally crossed the finish line. God knew exactly the kind of husband I needed when He gave me you all those years ago. You are the steady in my life. From the beginning of our marriage in 2007, you have been strong, faithful, and brave enough to hold my hand in every season of life, especially in this season of writing my very first book. It hasn't always been easy, but together you helped me fight off the lies of the enemy and called me an author even when I didn't fully believe it. In the midst of it all, you have truly held my hand through this work of my heart and even through the frustrations and near point of tears when I wanted to quit. Thank you for not letting me quit and for calling forth the gold in me. You are my rock next to Jesus—always have been and forever will be.

I love you so much my KISA.

To My Beth,

As a little twelve-year-old shy girl in youth group...you saw me. You saw my brokenness, you saw my heart, you saw my sadness, and you and Bill, as volunteer youth leaders, pursued me and never gave up on me. When I finally chose to trust you with my heart, you became my safe place, my sounding board, and my example of what love looks like in action. I watched you intently as you loved your children and Bill so well. I learned how to do family from you. I would not be the wife, mother, leader, spiritual mom, and lover of Jesus I am today without the life you spoke into me. You encouraged me not to give up, to rise above my circumstances, and to choose life again and again. Thank you for taking me under your wing and becoming the role model I so desperately needed. Though the years and miles have created distance, I carry with me the memories that shaped me—the bedtime tucks, pillows piled on my feet for bed, our late-night talks, warm cups of tea or coffee, your hugs, fun summer days and sweet summer evenings at Lake Wildwood, and the joy of simply doing life together. I treasure how after all these years, you are still in my life and that we can just pick up the phone or share an in-person hug from time to time and it feels like no time has passed. Words will never be enough to express my gratitude to God for placing you in my story. I honor you, Beth, for the godly woman you are and the eternal impact you've made in my life. This truly is a huge part of your spiritual legacy too!

I LOVE YOU!

P.S. Can't wait to see your BIG crown in Heaven!

To Gaudy (Gaudencia, My Sugarplum),

You were just a teen, and God put you in my home in Tanzania. You will always hold a special place in my heart as my first spiritual daughter. In you, I often recognized glimpses of myself as an overcomer, a longing for more of God, a deep hunger for His fire, choosing to live a life of victory despite painful experiences. Out of our journey together, I came to recognize the great need for spiritual mothers and fathers to rise up, to speak to the broken places, to be restorers of hope, and to pour courage into the next generation. You, dear Dada, are my living testimony of breakthrough. The woman you are today—the devoted and faithful wife, the amazing sweet mother, the wise and powerful spiritual mother—shines with such beauty and strength. Your life is a reminder that love, discipleship, and obedience to God truly transforms lives, and I am in awe of the story God is writing through your life. Though continents separate us now, I will always hold a special place in my heart for you.

I love you deeply, Dada, and I am endlessly proud of you!

To Allie, My Spiritual Daughter and My Armor Bearer,

You have been more than a just a support to me, you have been a gift from God, a steady strength, and a safe place in my journey. I'm grateful to God that He spoke to you to be my armor bearer, a role you haven't taken lightly. An armor bearer in the old days was chosen to carry the weight of the warrior's armor and stand faithfully in battle. That is exactly what you have done for me. You have come alongside me and helped carry burdens, you fought when I was weary, and stood in the gap when I felt I had nothing left to give. You've been my right hand while building Roaring Hope and my loyal confidant in life.

Allie, you are a warrior in your own right. You fought for your own breakthrough, and then you let me walk with you into greater freedom. Watching you grow into who you are called to be as an author, teacher, speaker, prophetic voice, and so much more has been one of the greatest joys in my life. Thank you for your *yes*.

I will never forget the way you helped carry me through some of the hardest valleys of my life. When my sister was dying, you drove me 2.5 hours each way, day in and day out to be by her side, never letting me walk that road alone. You sat with me in grief and helped give me strength in one of the saddest times of my life. You stood by my side in Colorado, knowing that trip would carry more weight than grief. It was an assignment from God to forgive my father and release him from shame in person. You got to meet him when even my own husband and children didn't, and you were there as a witness to one of the most powerful God moments in my life. You were with me in North Carolina when I resigned after 16 years as a missionary and 21 years as a licensed minister under Fire International. That day closed one chapter of my life and opened another, and you were covering me with your love, strength, and prayers through it all.

We've had our differences, and we have fought for brave communication through the years, yet in the hard, frustrating moments, we chose to keep our love on with each other. In doing so, trust was forged—stronger and deeper, day by day.

Allie, you've done life with me in the raw, the painful, and the holy moments. You have stood with me, carried me, and covered me, and this book is proof of how you do this so well. Thank you for being the "doula" to this book—for carrying it, pushing with me, and helping it be born. With your help, this book crossed the finish line, and I know this is just the beginning of more to come. GET READY! Together, we have more lives to reach, more books to write, and so much more to ensure Heaven is fuller and hell is emptier.

Allie, I'm forever grateful for you. I love you deeply, and I am so proud of the woman you are and the woman you're becoming. Watching you blossom is my joy! I love you.

Mama Mary (AKA: Boss Lady)

Friend, I am excited for you to step out in faith and grow a tree of legacy. It all starts with sonship. True sons and daughters love to climb in their Father's lap and feel their Father's embrace, and they can just *be*. I have created a special playlist for you. Scan the QR code below for a playlist of worship songs that will bring you into the presence of God.

I highly encourage you to take time with the Lord and journal each day. As you listen and worship, write what He says to you, or simply just lay and rest in Him. Friend, I promise you He is excited and waiting. Get ready for heavenly encounters.

About The Author

Mary L. Street was born and raised in the Bay Area of California. As a child, Mary met the Lord at a kid's camp and dedicated her life to Him despite the difficulties of her upbringing and home life. She passionately loves the Lord and pursues Him wherever He leads her. A supernatural encounter with the Lord in 1996 during the Brownsville Revival in Pensacola, Florida, radically touched her life and set her on fire for Him, and she hasn't been the same since.

Mary's huge heart for the nations led her to fulltime missions work in Tanzania, Africa, in 2003 at the young age of 27. There, she met her wonderful husband, Peter. Together, Mary and Peter have four beautiful children.

Mary served in Tanzania, Africa, for 16 years in missions until the Lord called her and her family back to the USA where He began to stir and grow bigger dreams in her heart. While missions is still a big part of her focus, she is also a business owner, ministry leader, author, speaker, and life coach.

While she loves speaking into and discipling the younger generation, Mary is passionate about pulling the gold out of people of all ages, seeing them step into their *full* identity as sons and daughters of God. She lives from a place of big faith and knows the reality that nothing is impossible with God!

For more information or to book Mary for your event, visit:

www.roaringhope.com.

About Roaring Hope International

Roaring Hope exists to bring transformational life to the hearts of people globally by working together with our partners, touching one life at a time.

We are committed to empowering people, creating family for the orphan, healing for the broken hearted, and bringing freedom to those in bondage.

We equip people with hope, joy, and confidence by teaching them how to step into their full identity in Jesus Christ. We are called to raise up leaders and see them impact the world.

We believe that when people know who they are and ***whose*** they are, anything is possible.

Check out our website now at **www.roaringhope.com**.

We also have a podcast called *Roar Out Loud,* which you can check out by scanning the QR code below.

End Notes

Introduction
Page 22: Matthew 13:31–32 NASB1995
Page 22: Cultivating Mustard Seed Faith
https://en.wikipedia.org/wiki/Mustard_(condiment)
Page 22: The Fragrant Garden By: Gwen Johansson
https://thefragrantgarden.com/mustard-tree-facts/
Page 23: Ezekiel 47:12 – Reference
Page 23: Matthew 17:20 – Reference
Page 25: Summary By: Vivian Tuong www.americanexpress.com/en-us/business/trends-and-insights/articles/6-incredible-companies-that-started-in-a-garage/
Page 25: Wikipedia https://en.wikipedia.org/wiki/Apple_Inc.
Page 25: Style / By Luxury Columnist: 21 Most famous Painters in the World
https://luxurycolumnist.com/most-famous-painters-in-the-world/
Page 26: Matthew 19:26 – Reference
Page 27: Romans 15:13 NASB1995

Chapter 1
Page 32: Matthew 18:3–4 NASB1995
Page 35: Matthew 19:36 – Reference
Page 35: 2 Corinthians 5:17 ESV
Page 35: Revelation 21:19–20 – Reference
Page 35: Matthew 7:9 – Reference
Page 35: Psalm 127:2 AMP
Page 35: Genesis 1:26 – Reference
Page 35: Psalm 139:14 – Reference
Page 36: John 8:44 – Reference
Page 36: 2 Corinthians 3:18 – Reference

Chapter 2
Page 37: www.biblestudytools.com/bible-study/topical-studies/forgiveness-the-very-essence-of-our-faith-11639431.html
Page 38: Luke 15:3–7 – Reference

Page 40: Psalm 33:5 – Reference
Page 40: 2 Thessalonians 1:6–8 – Reference
Page 40: Matthew 18:6 – Reference
Page 40: Romans 12:19 – Reference
Page 40: Matthew 18:21–22 NASB1995
Page 40: Colossians 3:13 NLT
Page 40: Breaking Free of Chains of Chains of Unforgiveness and Bitterness, By: Erica Ord; August 7, 2020 – https://uncaggedbird.com/breaking-free-of-the-chains-of-unforgiveness-and-bitterness/
Page 44: Romans 2:4 – Reference
Page 44: Matthew 18:35 – Reference

Chapter 3
Page 52: *Smith Wigglesworth Devotional: 365-Day Devotional* – ISBN 9780883685747 – Page 292 June 30
Page 55: Matthew 14:13–21 – Reference
Page 55: 1 Kings 17:8–24 – Reference

Chapter 4
Page 59: Hebrews 11:1 NASB2020
Page 60: Psalm 139:7–8 NIV
Page 60: John 8:32 – Reference
Page 61: 1 Kings 3:9 ESV
Page 61: Knowing Scripture/ Exegetical Note: A Hearing Heart (1 Kings 3:9) By: Daniel Hoffman; https://knowingscripture.com/articles/a-hearing-heart-1-kings-3-9
Page 61: 1 Kings 3:11 ESV
Page 61: 1 Kings 3:9, 11 ESV
Page 63: Philippians 4:13 NKJV
Page 63: Proverbs 18:21 NIV
Page 63: James 3:4–5 – Reference
Page 64: Romans 12:2 NASB1995
Page 66: Proverbs 18:21 NIV
Page 67: The Neuroscience of change: How to train your brain to create better habits, by: Thomas Oppong; June 25, 2018 www.theladders.com/career-advice/the-neuroscience-of-change-how-to-train-your-brain-to-create-better-habits

Chapter 5

Page 69: Hebrews – Reference
Page 70: Genesis 6:9–9:28 – Reference
Page 70: 1 Samuel 17:38–53 – Reference
Page 70: Judges 7:4–16 – Reference
Page 70: Luke 1:26–56 – Reference
Page 70: www.beliefnet.com/faiths/christianity/the-8-most-important-women-of-the-bible.aspx?p=3
Page 70: Fear of Man references:
https://encyclopediabc.wordpress.com/2019/07/11/fear-of-man-2/
Page 71: Ruth 2–Ruth 4 – Reference
Page 71: Esther 1–Esther 10 – Reference
Page 71: Hebrews 11 – Reference
Page 72: Exodus 2:1–10 NASB1995
Page 73: Exodus 6:20 NASB1995
Page 73: Numbers 26:59 NASB1995
Page 74: Hebrews 11:23 – Reference
Page 74: Exodus 2:2 – Reference
Page 74: Acts 7:20 – Reference
Page 74: Hebrews 11:23 – Reference
Page 75: https://travel2egypt.org/are-there-crocodiles-in-the-nile/
Page 76: John 11:35 – Reference

Chapter 6

Page 79: Philippians 4:13 NKJV
Page 80: Fear of man definition www.instagram.com/p/DDFck4mvBfb/
Page 80: When People Are Big And God Is Small by Edward Welch
Page 80: Proverbs 29:25 NASB1995
Page 84: Proverbs 23:7 NKJV
Page 84: Psalm 34:18 NASB1995
Page 84: Isaiah 61:1–3 NASB1995

Chapter 7

Page 92: Revelation 12:11 NASB1995
Page 93: Acts 10:15–16 – Reference
Page 93: John 2:1–12 – Reference
Page 93: Matthew 5:1–12 – Reference
Page 94: Matthew 10:7-8 – Reference

Page 95: John 14:14 – Reference

Chapter 8
Page 106: Matthew 7:9–11 NASB1995
Page 106: Numbers 23:19 – Reference

Chapter 9
Page 110: Genesis 35:15 – Reference
Page 110: Joshua 4:1–8 – Reference
Page 111: James 1:2-3 NIV
Page 112: James 1:6–8 ESV

Chapter 10
Page 120: Joshua 24:15 NASB1995
Page 122: John 14:12 – Reference
Page 122: John 14:12 NASB1995
Page 123: Proverbs 18:21 – Reference
Page 123: Deuteronomy 28:13 – Reference

Chapter 11
Page 125: 2 Corinthians 1:20 NASB1995
Page 125: Isaiah 55:11 NASB1995
Page 126: Jeremiah 29:13 – Reference
Page 129: John 14:13–14 NASB1995

Prayer Into Great Faith
Page 132: Jeremiah 17:7–8 NASB1995
Page 133: John 1:12 NASB1995
Page 133: John 3:16 NASB1995
Page 133: Romans 10:9 NASB1995

www.ingramcontent.com/pod-product-compliance
Lightning Source LLC
LaVergne TN
LVHW020715110826
845149LV00012B/2271